DRUN IN A MIDNIGHT CHOIR

volume 1
welcome to the new hallelujah

DRUNK IN A MIDNIGHT CHOIR VOL. 1

Welcome to the New Hallelujah

We have tried in our way to be free.

Book Design: Melissa Newman-Evans

Edited by: Todd Gleason, Eirean Bradley, William James, Chillbear Latrigue, Adam Tedesco

MASTHEAD:

Editor-El-Heifer: Todd Gleason
Curator of Poetic Badassery: Eirean Bradley
Wordsmoker Liaison/Highly Imposing Man/Vidster: Chillbear Latrigue
Punk-Rawk Loco-Motivator of the Musikal Maestros: William James
Grand Inquisitor: Adam Tedesco
Prettiness Engineer: Melissa Newman-Evans
Ghost in the Machine: Tommy

TABLE OF CONTENTS

FOREWORD

I used to write plays. Mostly in high school and college, and a few after. A handful of them were produced, but mercifully, the earliest ones are lost to history, except in memories, or maybe on some VHS tape in a box in somebody's parents' basement, that no one (thank God) will ever bother to watch. I cringe when I recall certain snippets of dialogue, and the yappy, pseudo-cool, pop-culture obsessed, urban-myth-laced influence of early Quentin Tarantino. I also had a terrible habit of writing long scenes where everybody in the cast sat around on couches trying to sound clever and arguing about nothing particularly important, until two of the characters finally came to blows. It didn't help that I was all too comfortable writing way above my weight class—about marriage and war and the Civil Rights movement and being a professional artist—all as I was still living on microwave burritos, bouncing around in mosh pits, and using student loan money to buy weed and sixers of Mickey's Big Mouth while my phone (yes, a land line) was about to get shut off for the fifth time. The plays had to be excruciating for actual adults to watch, but for whatever reason they kept encouraging me to stick with it, so I did.

What kept me coming back, what I personally found so exciting about writing plays was watching my words come to life right in front of me. I handed over the script and soon enough there was music and sets and actual people on stage, speaking dialogue I had written, and fighting and kissing and crying, just the way I had imagined them doing. Of course, these were students and amateurs for the most part, and so, as you can imagine, my painfully amateurish writing performed by relatively inexperienced actors produced some less than transcendent theatrical moments. However, there were those rare moments where something ignited—some flicker of violence or truth or laughter that came alive on the stage—and you could feel the crackle of real theater happening.

This invariably had less to do with my writing than with some choice the actor or director had made that breathed genuine vigor into that moment. It was no longer mine. Once I finished the script, the production took on a life of its own, a beast that, for good or for ill, had grown completely beyond my control. It was exhilarating and terrifying, and sometimes made me sick to my stomach or on the verge of tears or filled with unnameable joy—sometimes all three at once.

I'm not sure there was much actual art happening. But what was happening for me was that I was learning to sit at the edge of my creations, like at the edge of a campfire, and let them burn themselves wildly up into the fabric of night.

Drunk In A Midnight Choir (drunkinamidnightchoir.com) was just a glimmer of an idea for a long time. I wrote with characteristic verbosity (which I am trying my best to avoid here, I promise) about the original inspiration in an essay titled "The Big Sink," but in short, I wanted a place for my writing that felt like home—some clean, well-lighted place that didn't take itself too seriously, that didn't feel like it had walls all around it, with the VIPs inside and everybody else on the outside. I just wanted to create, and I wanted others to create with me. I didn't intend to start a blog to host nothing more than a collection of my daily rants and musings. What interested me was community, but communities aren't conjured out of thin air. They grow organically, by attracting individuals with a shared sense of purpose and values. A creative community has a life of its own that is exponentially more powerful than the singular voice and taste of one measly editor.

In the beginning, I had plenty of ideas and notions about what I wanted DMC to be. Some came to pass, a lot of others didn't. And many, many better ideas came along from other smarter, more talented people. The whole beast has been shaped by the voices, desires, struggles, and dreams of our community of editors and writers and readers. And what a beautiful little beast it is! It's pure magic watching it grow and become, and it has done so beyond my wildest expectations, thanks to so many incredibly talented, generous-hearted contributors. DMC would simply not exist, in any form worth reading, without them.

Oh, we're scrappy, all right. We are not a slick outfit. We've got untrimmed beards, calloused hands, mismatched socks, duct-taped shoes, and crumbs all over the keyboard. Which, please don't misunderstand me, is not some attempt to claim a bit of "authenticity." I couldn't give less of a fuck about authenticity. All it means is we don't care what kind of raw deal we got or you got or we gave ourselves, or how creaky our bones are, how broken our hearts, how dissonant our thoughts, how empty our pockets, or how many bootheels are trying to press us into the pavement—we're reaching for the fucking stars. And we know if we all just lift each other a little higher, we'll get there. Someday. Together.

What you hold in your hands is just a sliver of the amazing work we were fortunate enough to publish on the site over the last year and a half, as well as numerous pieces exclusive to this book. I am immensely grateful to all who have written, edited, read, submitted, donated, commented, "liked" our Facebook page, and shared our posts. I am grateful to you for reading these words. I am particularly grateful to Eirean Bradley,

Chillbear Latrigue, William James, Melissa Newman-Evans, and Adam Tedesco for their hard work, kick-ass taste, immense talent, diplomatic finesse, and boundless enthusiasm. Melissa Newman-Evans gets extra props for doing such a bang-up job of designing and formatting this book, guiding the rest of us through the process, and generally making us all look better than we deserve. Another special thanks to Tommy, Melissa Chandler, Amie Zimmerman, and Lauren Frament, who, along with Chillbear and Eirean, had the guts, the faith, and the generosity to jump on board with me, and be part of the site launch on February 6, 2014. Thank you Michael Heald (*Perfect Day Publishing*) and Carrie Seitzinger (*NAILED Magazine, Small Doggies Press*) for your time, generosity, and sound advice. And of course, my eternal thanks to Rebecca Wood, who so many times over the last 18 months, sat ever so patiently in the same room with me, as I sweated and swore at my computer, trying to wrestle yet another stubborn line of HTML into submission, never once uttered anything but kind and loving words, and who has the ability to read anything out loud and make it sound like it was written by a genius (great for a writer, not always for an editor).

So welcome to the new Hallelujah. This is our song. One song among many.

In spite of ourselves, we're romantics till we die. And sick, jaded bastards. Fighters for truth and liars for art. Cross-eyed, crazy, quick with a laugh or a kiss or a *fuck off*, we know what it's like to be picked last, and we'll never settle for it again. We've found hope and we've found guts. We've found the pill and it's called poetry. It's called community.

It's called The Choir.

-Todd Gleason

EIREAN BRADLEY

is a 2 time pushcart prize nominated author of 2 full length books of poetry "the i in team" and "the little big book of go kill yourself" on University of Hell Press. He is also the poetry curator on this lovely site. If you think this site sucks, he thinks you are wrong.

A Field Guide To Being Day Drunk In Your Hometown

Distance did not make the heart grow fonder.
Maybe Whiskey will.

Everyone here is not an ex, they do not need to be apologized to.

Hold your expatriate chin up proudly.

Tip the bartender if he assumes you are not from around here.
Tip double if he feigns awe at the liberal Shangri-La you have tumbled from.

You are WORLDLY now.

Even if it is ten degrees too warm for your hoodie, cling to it. It is your coat of arms.
It is your shield. It is the Tartan that your people will recognize you by. You are NOT in
Rome, so ignore the short sleeves of your day drinking companions, you do not have to
do what they do.

Whiskey has not worked yet.

Order a draft beer from your adopted region in its local colloquial way: Oly, beast, Star,
Gansett, Ronyay, etc. etc.

Express shock, but accept your hi-life with grace and tip the heathen anyway.

Acceptable reading material: Bukowski, Nick Flynn, James Baldwin, Dorothy Parker,
The Economist, or the New York Times.
Even pretending to read is acceptably impressive.

Even at your most depressed you have not wanted to commit suicide as badly as the
wood paneling in this bar does.

If you choose to do the crossword, make sure that none of the other patrons can see
that you keep continuously writing "ohgod" in all of the five letter options.

Keep drinking until the idea of tattooing a boomerang on your neck goes away. Your
situation is only temporary. You are above this.

Do not let the other patrons see you unfavorably comparing them to what their day
drinking counterparts in your dearly missed golden city look like. It is not their fault that
they are not the straight backed, porcelain toothed, ample breasted or sturdy chested

sophisticates you normally rub elbows with. It is not their fault that evolution doesn't happen to everyone.

The jukebox IS YOUR ENEMY. Unless you enjoy disappointment.

They still only serve hi-life on tap here.

Consider ordering a drink that best exemplifies the feeling of being back here. Scratch that. There is no liquor that tastes as much like ashes as your mouth does at this moment.

Everyone here reminds you of someone you have failed at one point.
Everyone here reminds you of someone you have fucked at one point.

APOLOGIZE
TO
NO
ONE.

Apology is so
small
town.

You would get up to leave but this city is a forest   of sharpened corners.

The whiskey is working on everything   but the whole heart/fonder part.

Ask both   bartenders for just one drink to file down all the edges.

You never noticed before   how the sidewalks
                         here are the same color as old bone   and decaying inci-
sors.

Your accent is   coming back.
                         That is why EVERYONE   IS looking at you.
That is why.

Even the sun is embarrassed about being here.   ALL it wants is Super Nova.
The sun wishes it had a face   so it could hide that face in shame.

There are TEETH

                                        everywhere.

Silly Child, You have to be a prisoner first to escape.

escape.

Look around   slowly.

All your ghosts are HERE. Just where   you left them.

They missed you.

Look.   Look.   Look.

Look.

Their arms are outstretched to touch you, THEIR MOUTHS ARE OPEN to receive you as you drift   down to join them.

You have always been
    welcome here.

You Always Thought The Music InYour Hometown Sounded Ominous

the bouncer will embrace you,

former coworker of Ian's, Megan's exboyfriend,
that guy you kicked out of the coffeeshop
for shooting up in the bathroom on a Monday afternoon, but still
a good enough guy.

He will use the meat of his uninvolved fist
to tenderize your back a little too aggressively.

Thirty seconds after asking where you've been,
why you ghosted,
the "hey, you lost weight" when you haven't,
the "did you know my ex moved to Portland right after you?", when you didn't,
the "it's been 10 years right?", when you are keenly aware of time/distance,
He will ask if you heard what happened to _____.

She is dead.
_____ is also,
got into a drunk driving accident with_____
They were reincarnated as page 4 headlines,
guest stars in a defensive driving video that teenagers are forced to watch.

_____ and _____ and _____ overdosed;
_____ is in jail.

_____ became a paper mache version of himself in hospice.

The cops found _____ after she had been dead for a week,
Her roommate had been out of town.
The bouncer will tell you about the smell, the fumigation process,
how the roommate slept on his couch,
how she still owes him a hundred bucks, and how
_____ and _____ got divorced after
the miscarriage, you heard about that right?

You will stand there with your shiver,
your matching set of newly shaking hands
smoking your cigarette,
when he says

"good to see you, hey, Megan's coming back to town in a coupla weeks,
we're gonna throw a rager at Dylan's , you know Dylan? he was _____ 's boy-
friend.
you should come, Megs will be so stoked to see you. It's been so long.

we thought you might have died."

To My Son On His Eighteenth Birthday

By now, it has become apparent to you
that you come from a lineage of highly unremarkable men.

There are endless things you have been given.
The winning ticket in the genetic lottery
was not in your gift basket.

I am not sorry for that.

You have inherited a bouquet of physical imperfections,
a litany from the book of "average".

You have also inherited your grandfather's smile,
his willingness to view people as infinite wonders,
his fearlessness and grace.

You have inherited your father's questionable fashion sense,
his fourteen left feet in the dancemoves department.

The fact that you most likely disagreed with that last line
means that you also inherited your father's
advanced abilities in the art of self delusion.

No, you are not exceptional by birth.
that part will have to be accomplished by you.

Do not worship at the altar
of the Church of Close Enough.

You were named your name.
You were not named Could've Been or Never Was.

There will be people who do less than you with more.
There will be people who do more than you with more.
There will be people who make your grasping and failures
look like grasping and failure.
Do not let them change your name to Bitterness.

There will be days that it is easier to be anything other
than you the man you are meant to be.

Remember that often the easiest things are the cheapest, the flimsiest, that they will dissolve as easily as they arrived.

There will be days that All The Good Guys Lose.
There will be days that The End Is Extremely Fucking Nigh.
There will be days that ugly Is the world's currency and mother tongue.

You will see evil.
you will see injustice smile at you with impossibly perfect teeth.
Bad things will happen to good people for no reason.
People you love will die.

Do not let it turn you mean.
Do not let it close your mouth.
Do not let it curl your open hands into fists.
Do not let it close you.

That is not who you are.
You were named your name.
When you were born your hands were unfurled and gloriously outstretched.
You were trying to pull the world in.

I know.
I was there.

The measure of a good man is not how hard he loves the world
It is how hard he loves the world even when he is sure the world
does not love him back.

There is nothing scarier than loving until your bones ache and crack
when that love may not be returned without your blood caked on it.

Remember that that which does not kill you,
Does Not Kill You.

Do not be frightened.
That is not your name.

Remember that you come from a lineage
of highly unremarkable men
who did not give you the keys to an easy, blameless life.

We gave you the best thing our limited bodies could carry.

Your grandfather carried it for you.
Your father carried it to you.
You are carrying our name.
You are carrying yours.

TONY BROWN

is a self-employed writer and consultant who lives in Worcester, MA. He's been do-
ing the poetry thing for close to 50 years. Also fronts the poetry and music band, "The
Duende Project," in which he does the poetry thing while posing now and then with a
guitar in front of three real musicians who make him sound badass, because THEY are
total badasses.

Ten Poems You Could Be Writing

1.

The one where you are speaking to one person you've never met in a dark room.

2.

The one recited from behind a white screen. You're backlit in Yankee Stadium on a small stage. There's no microphone, no public address system; the stadium is empty.

3.

The one like the previous one except you have the greatest sound system in world history. The stadium is still empty.

4.

The one where you ask the audience to harm you.

5.

The one where you speak through a gag -- a sleeve cut off a fresh corpse.

6.

The one in which you speak English but are trying to imitate the sound of another tongue, the one your grandmother spoke. Not a translation; English words that sound like the words she used. (Can you hear her?)

7.

The one in which you are completely fictional -- you were never born, all the memory you've got is false, and your audience will be surprised to discover you're not a beloved character from their favorite childhood book.

8.

The one in which the pen suddenly leaps out of your hand and stakes a territorial claim like a bear.

9.

The one in which the detective has not eaten for hours under the single white bulb, there is sweat, you are about to confess and it dawns upon you that lying or telling the truth doesn't matter as long as you can't smell your body emptying itself into this ill-fit suit, this outfit made for a coffin outing. You can't tell where you are, but it's a city you should have been born in. Your grandmother's coming to throw your bail. (Can you hear her? She's looking for you. Calling you. Asking for you by a name you never heard before, but it's yours.)

10.

The one where you are finally in a full stadium. There are lions.

Whiteness

I've taken to calling it
"Whiteness," that
low hum,
that cloud of unknowing.
It just keeps running.
I don't know how to turn it off.
It's caused amnesia
at a cellular level.
Try to put a finger on Whiteness
and it slides away
like mercury:
liquid, metal, baffling.
If I spoke magic I'd conjure it thus
and try to hold it still: come, be bound,
tsunami of broken mirrors,
snowfield of washed crosses,
tangle of lilies, thicket of oleanders,
angular dramas, spoiled seeds...
Can you truly say
it is not its own distinct thing?
It cannot be defined any longer
as absence or default.
If I stare into Whiteness
long enough and hard enough
I lose myself in it -- no surprise;
it was built in such a way
that one can't help
but stare into it:
the far end
of a hall
of locked doors.
A television permanently tuned
to a news station that promises
your story will be read soon,
right after this word,
right after this word from our sponsor.
It's not about the nature
of individuals, exactly,
except when it is --
except when
one of them doesn't see how

they're soaking in it;
except when they call it
"the norm"
to cancel out
"the other."
It's not about how hard or soft
someone has
or hasn't had it, exactly,
except when it is --
except when
it silently opens a stuck door
and things are even a touch easier
for someone who denies
or doesn't even realize that they
carry that key with them everywhere.
It's not about
anything other than
itself, really, and that
is the problem: how
slippery it is
with its privileges, how slick it is
without admitting it,
how invisible it is to itself.
But I can see it tonight
as I stand under the eaves
of my father's house, rain coming down
just beyond my nose; there's
Whiteness in my face, in my ear,
in my blood, all over me
whispering,
be one with me...
I don't know.
Maybe
it's that flag
of bones it's wrapped in,
maybe it's knowing how many bones
were abandoned
in deserts far and near
under that flag,
maybe it's knowing
how many bones drifted down
to the seabeds
of the Middle Passage.
Maybe it's

the long goodbye
I'd have to make
to my otherness
once I accept
the name for my own,
or maybe it goes back, all the way back
to those childhood Saturdays
where the question at playtime
was always
whether I wanted to be the cowboy
or the Indian
and I always chose what felt closest.
It was fine until
one day
someone asked
why I always wanted
to be the bad guy
and never
the cowboy.
Hello, Whiteness,
is what I should have said then
but I was young and uneasy,
afraid not to play along.
I hung up my cap guns
soon after that for safety's sake --
but we were just getting started,
Whiteness and me.
Whiteness started haunting me, needling me,
kept repeating:
why do you always want
to be the bad guy?
in that supple voice.
It spit that
a million different ways
and they all meant the same:
why celebrate
difference? why you gotta
be like that? calm down
and sink into me
like you would a milk bath,
like you would surrender to
a horizon wiping blizzard.
Go to sleep. I promise
it will be warmer

eventually.
That voice eventually faded into
a low hum, a cloud of unknowing.
Whiteness, let me tell you,
maybe I'm wrong,
maybe it's amnesia
at a cellular level,
but maybe I fear you so much
because
I can't recall anyone
ever saying
it made them warmer
to die a little.

Cryptozoology

So, there's this website where you click to spin a wheel
and it tells you how to make a life decision
based on you doing what a unicorn would do
if a unicorn was in the same situation you're facing.
I spun the wheel this morning
and it said I should
"whinny and rear."
Well, I do this all the time so it didn't seem to be a huge stretch.
I was glad I was not advised to nuzzle a newborn or frolic in a meadow.
I was hoping that I'd be told to impale evil things
but I confess I'm not really in shape for that.
(Good call, wheel.)
So: out the front door on my hind legs,
waving my arms around.
My voice has too much tobacco in it for a solid whinny,
but I made some sort of approximate noise
as I went forth.
At the gas station, the pump refused my credit card. I whinnied at it.
There wasn't much space to rear since I'd parked too close to the pump,
but I managed something that didn't look too un-unicorn-like
and fulfilled the prophecy. I was becoming mythical!
Certainly, the pump's refusal to honor my credit made that belief credible.
I drove out to the Tower Hills, just outside the city.
I knew I'd be the lone unicorn out there, since it's not the season for the regular uni-
corns --
while they equally adore frolicking in meadows covered in snow or wildflowers,
the mud of a Massachusetts spring is something they'd rather not touch.
They go to Arizona, I think, in winter.
I pulled off the road by the reservoir
and found a trail there,
which I followed to a bar
in a clearing.
The bar was better furnished than I would have expected,
and the drinks were well made and cheap.
The bartender greeted me with a nod;
apparently I had been there before,
though it all seemed new.
I knew no one else,
at least by their faces,
though I recognized them by their traits --
gryphons whose wings had been stolen,

chimeras with odd parts from random plastic surgeries,
basilisks who could turn you to Corian with a single glance.
I joined my fellow cryptids there
and we indulged in our fortunes
for many, many hours
until I was drunk on the dizzying rhythm
of my whinnying and rearing.
I came home flecked with sweat
and exhausted. I dreamed of virgins
seeking me, I dreamed of eluding capture --
and then I woke up -- here. Again.
I'm going to return
to that website with its majestic wheel.
It tells me old stories
that make me feel like I'm not alone
in believing that there's a greater purpose.
I know it's supposed to be for amusement only,
but it's a joke
that has led me to a place
where I feel almost verified
and almost at home.

MELISSA CHANDLER

lives and writes in San Francisco where things are gettin bananas. She's on Twitter @melchandler

Alexander Schmalexander Jones

Everyone always said Alexander Schmalexander Jones had nine lives. Probably he had more; I don't think he ever counted. Here are some I know: As a baby, Alexander jumped off the roof of his house and lived. As a child, he put stones in his pockets and floated. One humid summer day, Alexander and his one true junior high love took turns poisoning each other with everything they had around: insect spray stirred into chocolate milk, pills from their mothers' purses crushed and deposited into peanut butter sandwiches. These episodes resulted in a lot of vomiting and even a trip to the ER where Alexander had to drink a charcoal to hedge against kidney damage, but he didn't die. His one true junior high love held his hand and looked at his test results hanging on the wall as if they were graven images.

In high school, Alexander wrapped his car around a tree and crawled right out through the shattered window. (He didn't wreck because he was drunk; he wrecked because his idiot friend burned him on the back of his neck with a pipe). He carried his dead idiot friend for two miles down that road by the time a car passed by to help. Later he climbed through the window and got into the bed of his one true high school love and cried and cried for his idiot friend and for idiocy in general and death, and his one true high school love lay beside him and stroked his hair and caught his tears on her fingers. When it was time to go and Alexander crawled back out the window, he wished he was crawling back in through the window of his demolished car. He would stay there in the dark in the middle of the twisted, hot metal and he would do what it took to push and pull out his idiot friend before he started breathing the swarming black smoke that would smother him.

In college Alexander went skiing and was trapped under an avalanche for close to thirty minutes. When rescuers dug him out, he wasn't breathing anything but ice. He was thinking of his idiot friend from high school, as he did from time to time, and he was wondering if it was preferable to die by smoke or by ice. He wondered this purely out of curiosity, because he knew the cold that encased him now wouldn't kill him. Alexander believed he knew how he would die, so while his survival feats evoked wonderment and gratitude to others, none of them were much of any marvel to him.

Alexander wrote down his story for me while he was in a hotel in Paris, and it went like this:

I die in a huge amount of pain and alone, after falling down an open sewage grate on a dark street. Although I have witnessed the scene many times clearly in my mind, and am 100% certain that it accurately portends my doom, I am also certain that I will not be able to use this knowledge to guard against my demise by the mere act of avoiding stepping near sewage grates. That's just not how it works. Instinctively, of course, I'll watch out for them, but there will be that one sewage grate that will blindside me one day. Once I'm settled onto the floor of the sewer, with my back broken from where it bounced across a pipe, I'll lie curled at a strange angle in the dark. There will be no visions of lights or angels, just the grit of dirt and gravel between my fingers and the smell of the shit of a whole lot of people, and the sharp stabs of...

"Stop!" said his one true love. "Enough!" (I had been reading over his shoulder.)

Alexander put down his pen and grabbed me below the waist. He hoisted me over his shoulder and carried me to the bed. Every night in Paris we had wine and cheese for dinner and wine and cheese for dessert and walked until the cold wouldn't let us feel our hands and feet. The hotel was so warm. Every night in Paris was the best night anyone in the entire world ever had. Alexander accidentally pulled the plugged-in hair dryer into the hotel's bathtub while he was soaking, and electrocuted the hell out of himself, but he didn't die. He lived. He left Paris with welts across his back that looked like trees in winter, and later they turned to white scars. Alexander never finished the story of his death. I took it and hid it in a small pocket of my purse. Later at home I buried it in the yard.

He didn't die for a while. We had two children, a little girl and a little boy. When our little girl was thirteen she put rat poison in her boyfriend's frappe and Alexander and I shared knowing glances all the way to the hospital. When our little boy was twenty-two and not so little anymore, he jumped into a canal and pulled two teenagers out of a submerged SUV, one alive one dead. When the mayor recognized his courage on the local news stations, Alexander cried for his son and for his old idiot friend from high school and for idiocy in general and death.

When Alexander died, it was just walking home from the grocery store. They'd put a new sewage grate in on Sandy River Road, our road, and they'd forgotten to screw in the screws. It was winter. The streets were icy. He was an old man. When they pulled him out he was frozen and covered in shit.

You Will Have to Choose

Everyone, you must decide: cake or pie.
Once you have made your choice,
you will receive a lifetime supply
from one Fernando Almondine. Fernando's
banana cream will have you in throes, and long ago
he sold his soul for the secret ingredient
in his framboise chocolat.

The only catch is that if you choose cake,
you will lose someone very dear to you.
The only other catch is that if you choose pie,
there will be an explosion on a bus in a country
you have never been to. Likely no one you know
will be onboard. When a father carries the bodies
of his dead children through the streets, his words
will be mixed with wailing, and therefore unintelligibly
grief-garbled (though I assume you would not possess
the conversational ease of his language
to translate them in the first place.)

One concern you may have at this juncture:
is cheesecake a cake or a pie? It is a cake by name,
served in decidedly pie format. We leave
this to your best judgment.

Fernando's baked goods have swept the
nation. I venture you will be ecstatically surprised.
Of course, demand for our goods is expected to rise
once you've returned a verdict on cakes v. pies.
Therefore, if you know any young, punctual workers,
please send them our way with a resume.

Beginning now, you will have five minutes to decide,
though I assume the majority of you have already
done so. Keep in mind,
when faced with decisions under duress of stress,
results in the aftermath are best
when adhering to initial impulse.

That said, for you cake-eaters:
when your loved one has died, you will at first,

as you may expect, experience a state of shock.
Your shock, however, in this case
will quickly manifest itself in such a way
that you will have trouble remembering
your departed is dead, or possibly even
that he or she has ever lived, instead.

Example:
say his boots remain in their place at the door.
Try them on. Clomp around the house
for a number of minutes, leaving trails of the dirt
he gathered when he last walked. Make a mess!
As you unlace them, as you clean up,
you will experience not sadness
but a vaguely euphoric type of confusion,
significantly reducing any obligation
of active grief on your part.
And the boots will never run out of dirt.
And later you'll have your cake.

CORTNEY LAMAR CHARLESTON

    hails from the Chicago suburbs. A basketball fanatic, macaroni & cheese connoisseur and not-so-closeted anime lover, he spends a lot of time thinking about all the things he could be doing in that moment but isn't. While he's being pensive, his girlfriend is probably turning the TV to the *Real Housewives of Atlanta* or some other locale and he just goes with it; he may even like it at this point.

Hip-Hop Introspective #3

Ninth grader, and I'm still very unsure if sex is
the act or the idea. It's pitch black in my bedroom,
aside from *2:00 AM* blinking in red-digital spine
and *BET Uncut* on the TV screen.

I have the volume on mute, but my stomach
is audible, groaning with a new kind of empty,
watching her mocha-colored skin oscillate
at the thigh like hot coffee skimmed
by the blowing of an eager thirst.

Video after video, every Saturday and next,
my head is in the thick of her, of women, of sex,
maybe; the credit card swipes straight down
her thong-line, and I think to myself:

booty don't lie, jo.

Homies can lie about it sometimes, though. Even in
ninth grade, act: build personas on the firmness of it
like they got mixtapes to sell out the ass of a car.

But I know a rapper ain't always who he says he is;
and a wrapper ain't always for who he claims it is.

Truth is, in high school or anywhere, a *ho*
ain't nothing but rumor, a stretch of leg to fit
a forced rhyme scheme cause his tired lyrics
couldn't unwrap her at the seams, it seems to me.

I mean, I don't rap. With anybody; I feel
uncomfortable trying to grasp the supple parts
of languages romantic or explicit, don't know
where to start from and still remain real.

You know, real. Like the dopest rappers should be,
or golden wrappers, from what she and her be chirping
by the lockers, at the lunch table, within shot of my ear.
And all them boys be telling me *peep game. Respect
my Mars, man.* But I know the reel; get the idea,
I think: of her, of women, of sex, maybe?

Keeping JELL-O

"The Bill Cosby thing is so ... awful... It was a badly kept secret in the comedian world, and a lot of us would talk about it."

— *Patton Oswalt*

Being a highly processed food, it is built to last. If speaking to the pre-packaged gelatin that comes in plastic cups for individual serving, the product can last in a cold refrigerator anywhere from 12 to 18 months, should it remain factory sealed, and not many secrets can survive that long and still come out so shocking to the taste buds or whatever else. Opening them after the expiration date has passed does not inherently mean the product cannot be consumed, or provide some type of relief, but it may leave a poor taste in your mouth or elsewhere. If worried about taste, consider purchasing the powder mix and then stowing it away in a cool, dark pantry where it can sit indefinitely. When you finally open the package, do not be surprised if it looks like cremated remains, do not be alarmed if, after consuming, your tongue feels possessed, moves to recite names of women you've never heard of: this has been well-documented; it is a common reaction to have.

Natasha Romanoff Deactivates Her OkCupid Profile

A potential interest that suspiciously resembles a colleague she's been catching "vibes" from sends her a private message, outright calls her a *slut*. Now, that's story enough for anybody, but it doesn't stop there – he posts it on all his social channels as a caption to her picture, shouts it from rooftop bars across New York City with a megaphone, even buys billboard space in Times Square, TV commercials for his smear campaign: clearly well endowed. And suddenly nerds from all across the galaxy are asking themselves on message boards *what kind of a name is Black Widow anyway?* They try to fathom how many mouths she's married to earn such a sinister moniker, what shape her own lips have taken to make men sing for sweet mercy – some kind of red halo shining in the dark; they think any man can look into her muted eyes and find whatever secret they most want to know. One by one, they flood her inbox with their standard list of questions kept for third dates they never make it to:

Natasha, have you ever been in love?
Natasha, do you love me? Natasha,
how many men have you killed
and notched into you bed post? Natasha,
am I the best that you've ever had?

And Ms. Romanoff, to her credit, doesn't get aggressive at all, though were she a mirror, it'd be justified. Instead, she gets political, making treatise out of repurposed Joan Jett lyrics, acrobatic with her words, forceful but fluid enough not to admit a weapon against her, an assassin until the very end; but in the end, Black Widow is only a fictional character – a collection of stories written mostly by men. Nothing she says is true, factually speaking, and she knows this. Millions upon millions of avid comic book readers have been inside of her; she's felt them, crawling through her body at night like spider-men. They've tracked mud inside and chastised her for not learning how to kick without opening more space between her legs, still expecting her to win her fights, spill blood from everywhere but the one place anatomy designed for sacrifice, and so she goes off the grid, on a mission of her choosing, and ever since, when the wind blows through the trees, you can hear things snapping, one by one.

ROBERT DELAHANTY

Doing my best to live life doing what I love to do.

CALVIN
FANTONE

is a poet, educator, and amateur super villain. You can find him scheming in Orange County, California. He really wants to play video games with you.

Falling In Love With Oncoming Trains

It is not the tracks and their muted shine, not the gate
in its sluggish descent, or the warning bell's battered song.

It isn't the sweet blindness of night, city lights swallowed
by the dark's eager mouth, the wind drilling its secrets

through your bones, no. It's the shrill friction of wheels
attempting to rewrite the inevitable crash, the conductor's

frantic scramble for control. This is what drives you
forward. Not the whiskey and its gasoline anthems

tearing through blood vessels, its ugly shade of red
branching across your skin. Not the swimming pool

of pills behind your eyelids either, those elegant chemicals
rearranging everything. There is no more space inside you

for all that sickness, all that patient sinking. It's the longing
to be dressed in the wreckage like it's Sunday's best outfit;

it's the silence lodged in your withered throat. Your body
bracing for impact and travel, your body lusting for distance.

Facebook News Feed

after Rebecca Lindenberg

Calvin Fantone is off his medication again. Is staring out the window. Is thumbing through phonebooks, calling up strangers. Calvin would like to add you as a friend. Would like to add you as a friend. Would like to add you as a friend. Dances like he has thirteen left feet. Likes *impromptu dance parties*. Would like to switch on the music and add you as an impromptu dance partner. Daydreams about magic carpets. Nightdreams about sprouting wings. Likes *anthropomorphism*, likes *cryptozoology*. Calvin wonders what it would be like to mutate into a shooting star, the wishes of hundreds staplegunned to his body. Would like to add you as his velocity meter. In case he crashes through the atmosphere, Calvin would like you to be waiting on the ground with the world's largest trampoline. Would like to add you as a friend that owns a trampoline. Likes *junk food*. Is thankful for Taco Tuesdays. Would like to add you to the group, *WE LOVE TACO TUESDAYS NOMNOMNOM*. Has extremely high cholesterol. Calvin is a bloated shadow longing to shrink into a castle of light. Would like to add you to his brand new diet of matches and candles. Would like you to help him trim off the darkness. Calvin wants to be the grandest of floating pianos, music in the midnight sky. Wants to have conversations with the moon in the language of hammers and strings, hammers and strings, hammers and strings. Is scheming to transform. Calvin is an idea in infancy, a light bulb in a warehouse brimming with chandeliers. Would like to add you as a co-conspirator. Would like to add you as another light bulb flickering on, another light bulb becoming brilliant in the dark.

Jungle Turbulence

The guttural stammers of the chopper blade
punctuate the pilot's rhythm in the choppy tropic weather.
Just like playing chopsticks, he thinks, fingers floating across
the flight controls, but it's really Chopin's Allegro de Concert:
a piano's panicked rise and fall and rise in the storm, tempo all chopped up.
Sweat drips from the pilot's muttonchops, his grip begins to unsteady
itself. No one will find the wreckage hidden in all this unchopped jungle.
No one makes plans for dying ahead of time. Snippets of the pilot's life
he's forgotten hack their way through the fog of years in his mind—
the night he tore up his wedding photographs, his superior officer's
severed legs in the war, the morning he learned of his brother's death
from a newspaper clipping, his first lover's arms learning the shape
of sharpened steel. The pilot's mind is buried inside time's tears and creases.
He is cataloging his life. He is keeping it in pieces.

*first line taken from David Wojahn's, "It's Only Rock and Roll but I Like It -- The Fall of Saigon, 1975"

MCKENDY FILS-AIME

photo by Marshall Goff

hails from Manchester, New Hampshire, where he is an instrumental organizer and co-host for his home slam, the long-running and wildly popular Slam Free or Die. A seven-time veteran of the National Poetry Slam and perennial semi-finalist, as well as the winner of the Boston Poetry Slam's 2012 World Qualifier, he has been published in Freezeray, Word Riot, and Drunk in a Midnight Choir. The only thing Mckendy likes as much as poetry is his sneaker collection. He is currently working on his debut collection of poems, tentatively titled, *Prayer in the Cracks*.

For Those Who Whistle Vivaldi

You're standing in line at Walmart
holding a CD, watching a procession
of fitted caps.

Today 50 Cent's *Get Rich or Die Trying*
has been released & his fans are here.
Boys swallowed by their father's jeans,
sporting robe sized hoodies, praising the bullet
hole halo circling Curtis Jackson's crucifix.

It is the year you move to a town
where the people watch gangster rap videos
like National Geographic specials,
an anxious pearl mob clutching bags
& backing away when you approach.

You are the only dark skinned G-Unit monk here
so naturally the cashier is taken aback
when you hand her a copy of
The Johnson Academy presents:
Vivaldi's The Four Seasons

When she asks about the CD, you tell her
about the grocery clerk,
how you walked into his store,
headphones bumping Biggie
how the dark lure of you caught his eye.

In an aisle full of white kids, he patted you down,
hands alive with certainty. After he found
nothing, he told you to never come back.

You figured it was your music,
the slick rhymes spilling from your ears
riding a cavalcade of beats, stampeding
through the old man's best rendition of Spring.

You figured if you learned his song,
branded each note into your mouth
he'd let you back into the store.
He never did.

But that summer you stopped listening to Hip Hop
in public, wore nothing but dress shirts & khakis,
stocked up on Letterman jackets & college hoodies.
You told your language to pull its pants up,
to walk straight, to talk with respect.
You didn't want to seem too urban for your new town.

In 2010, Brent Staples coined the term
Whistling Vivaldi, recounting college days
when he'd hum classical music in public
to put the whites around him at ease.

But in Cambridge, black Harvard
professors still get arrested for going home.

In North Carolina, a college degree
won't stop a cop from emptying a clip
into an unarmed graduate.

In Detroit, an honor student's pleas
for help are only answered with shotgun.

You've been whistling Vivaldi your whole life
& even when you went to college
& got that good job
& wore clothes that fit
you have always sounded like a police siren to them.

Because no one gives a fuck
that violence is not your name,
that theft is not instinct,
that you were not born a sin.

They just want you to be a kerosene conductor,
a matchstick maestro, to play The Four Seasons
with ash & cinder, in the key of drive-bys.
Because fear is still this country's violin
& you are the scariest song in the show.

Prayer in the Cracks

It is cold & my arms are throwing
themselves into the air
like a southern Baptist church, grabbing
monkey bars like hallelujah.
I swear these hands can feel God.

If my mom were here she'd laugh,
praise me for this spectacle.
With every swing, I am praying,
though my body makes these bars
look more like an overturned "E"
than crucifix.

When I was seven, my mom
threw me a birthday party, invited
all my friends to our shanty apartment.

I wish I was still there, face stuffed
with a Power Rangers cake, vanilla
frosting hanging from my chin,
like a sugared Jesus.

Every Saturday night,
on our way to church,
a Hip Hop song's heavy bass
would move concrete, its tremor
quickening our pace.

On the way home, I'd run
into our building & watch the sun set
over the projects, wondering
if the rest of my life looked so broken.

This place wasn't built for religion
but we found pews in benches,
turned pedestrian bustle into mass,
made stained glass of barred windows.

In Spite of Heartbreak

In the weeks after you left,
I experimented with unmaking
myself. I filled my liver
with more booze than I drink
in a year, considered not stopping

for the frozen cars slithering
through rush hour traffic, tried losing
myself inside women who I fucked
like a manual on how to fuck you.
Before I taught myself how

to sleep alone again, I wrote
a poem on the fading pulse
of our relationship. It read:

Because your mouth creaks
the words "I love you," quiet
as an old shed's door, I know
you want me to leave. Because
my blood would rather circle
my body in solitude, I won't.
I have a list of reasons why
moving my things out our door
will become familiar.
I haven't shared them yet.
I'd rather be a small sound
in your throat than nothing.

After my parents divorced, my father stayed
in our old apartment where he lives
to this day. He's left everything the same
as if waiting for us to come home.

My mother is happily remarried.

Heartbreak only moves or does not
move us as much as we want it to.

When you finally say something
that doesn't sound like you've spent days

gargling it for consideration, you might find
me sitting on a park bench somewhere,
a collection of pruned limbs, layered
with tattered skin. My age, torn

pants pocket that youth falls out of,
the scattered chime of your absence
circling my feet. In these moments,
I must not let myself be a court jester
in the throne room of my own suffering.

I must not be a dusty belfry, waiting
to ring for an hour that may never come
again. Which is to say you may never

come again. I must remember that I am here,
and the years haven't left my body
and while your face is a fixture I haven't learned

to pull from the morning, each new sunrise
will push this pain back into me,
until it is ready to bloom
into something I can love more than you.

LAUREN ELMA FRAMENT

is a writer & feminist living in Manchester, NH. her biggest influences are Adrienne Droogas & Jeanna Fine. she likes cross-stitching & standing in the front at punk shows. follow her on twitter @sadsquatch_xo

for my father

who fell out of a treehouse he built
with his brothers. twelve years of boyhood,
hanging by a slice of his arm.

who swallowed a peach stone while driving
alone. how many years of unknowing,
how survival feels like choking.

who rode a motorcycle into a car, pavement
all winter & ice. eighteen years of daring Death,
not a single bone broken. not a scratch.

who fell off a tube tied to a moving boat, water
leading closed fist to face. how many years of loyalty—
wedding ring, a reminder gashed into his forehead.

who is fifty-nine years of sadness. who told me,
it's too late. there is no one who can help me now,
& believed it.

hampton street, 7:22 pm (prelude & chorus)

after Pyotr Ilyich Tchaikovsky's Symphony No. 2 in C minor, Op. 17

MVT. I: ANDANTE SOSTENUTO

everyone i've ever loved has held me like a grudge.
maybe i returned to him like he was the house
i grew up in—too many times, only hurting myself.
maybe i've just never been no enough.   never quite
shotgun, always more dart.   a near miss.   someone's
poor aim.

MVT. II: ANDANTINO MARZIALE

he wanted me to run away to Boston with him.
i was sitting on the bathroom counter, hugging my knees
so tight that my entire body became a clenched fist.
please. if you love me, you'll come with me.
but something held me there, a yearning
permanent fixture in that bathroom.

MVT. III: SCHERZO

years later, i will find a razor blade under the sink,
still just as sharp & reflective as the day it was born.
i will think i can draw him out of me;

i will only bleed.

MVT. IV: ALLEGRO VIVO

if you were to see me today,
you might not recognize me.   I've cut my hair.
turned vital, no longer just an empty pulse,
murmuring coffin resting among flatline
telephone wires.   I've cut my hair.
my name has not changed,
but it's said different now.

                                               I've cut my hair.
                                               I've cut my hair.`

43

the kind of silence that kisses you as if you have a real & honest mouth

after Heidi Therrien

& wasn't it how you wanted me—silent or roaring;
   bag of dogshit in flames on a porch /

& wasn't i a conduit of secrets (yours, not mine) /
   & didn't you want me quiet as blankets, a smothered undoing /

& didn't i eat my own words for half a year—
   a forced feast, everything looking stolen //

but weren't you also a lamp /
   & weren't you once close as a good mouth

(the shining accomplice to my leaving a bad man) /
   & didn't you listen then tell me nothing /

& wasn't the yellow brick road a two-way street /
   & haven't red shoes been a part of every woman's wardrobe /

& wasn't the great wizard just a plain man
   who knew how to talk right //

& wasn't your lie just a lie?
   & weren't you playing at smoke all along?

& now—what of now / aren't you
   just a tiny black hole of a ghost /

& your pen, a sad & empty word /
   & aren't you just a broken mirror

wearing how many faces // or a gaudy handbag
   full of dull & crooked teeth

TODD GLEASON

Editor-el-Heifer of DMC. Head Drunk. Big Sinker. John the Conqueroo. Like a knight from some old-fashioned book.

Remembering The Genie

In 1991, during my senior year in high school, I was lucky enough to win a grant from the Marin Education Fund for my writing and theater activities. I'd written some plays and directed one and acted in several and had served as Editor of the literary magazine for a few years and won a poetry prize. Honestly, none of it was really much of a big deal, and the work was of course all embarrassingly amateurish and awful, but I was pretty good at making it all sound impressive on paper. I didn't think I had much of a chance when I applied, but I somehow managed to snag one of the top prizes.

During the awards ceremony at our school, which had a large chunk of the winners, they read a short introduction for each of us. During mine, they quoted one of the judges, who had reportedly dubbed me "…maybe the most creative and talented person to ever attend this high school." I flinched when I heard that. It would have been nice to think she was right, but I couldn't even momentarily pretend that it was anywhere near the truth. I knew a handful of people in my class alone who were miles more talented, creative and accomplished than me– just maybe less good at showing off. Later, my theater teacher and mentor was beside herself over that. "What a terrible thing to tell someone," she laughed. "What were you thinking when you heard that?" I grinned and told her that at that moment I had happened to be looking right at the picture on the wall of Robin Williams in his Redwood High jacket. She liked that.

Robin Williams was our most famous alumnus, voted both "Funniest" and "Least Likely to Succeed" by his fellow students. Growing up, I grilled any one who had known him for stories, but rarely got any good dirt. Once, I had found a magazine with an article about celebrities in high school, and he was one of the features. It claimed he would shout "Good morning Redwood High!" every morning in the halls. I asked someone who had gone to school with him if that was true, and he frowned. "No way. C'mon. Nobody does stuff like that. That guy was such a geek. He wore bow-ties and was super quiet. I never liked him."

Well okay then. (Keep in mind that this was from one of the daytime regulars at The Silver Peso, who was also a small-time coke-slinger and all-around unreliable source.)

Robin's Redwood High yearbook photo had been used in *Dead Poets Society*, in the scene where the kids search the old manual to find information about their new teacher. During the summer before my junior year, that was the first movie I went to see with my soon-to-be first girlfriend. We both fell in love with that movie and we fell in love with each other while watching it and that would always be our movie. I felt connected to it in so many ways (not the least of which being that the character played by Ethan Hawke, my most convincing celebrity doppelganger, also shares my first name.) It spoke to my adolescent yearning and confusion, to my nascent search for meaning. The movie is as heavy-handed and sentimental as they come (not something likely to deter my overly sensitive 16 year-old self), but aside from Peter Weir's deft direction, the film is really saved by the pitch-perfect, heart-on-the-sleeve performance of its star. It was a classic role for him, allowing him, as his best ones did, to use all of his performer's tools, as well as showcase his range of personal qualities– from his wacky voices to his anarchic streak to his tender vulnerability to his utter, shining goodness. You have no doubt that this man genuinely wants to help these kids, to inspire them, to save them from the clutches of conformity, and this comes from the heart of the performer as much as anything. John Keating is the genuine article. And that's because Robin Williams is exponentially so.

Every recollection of him as a man mentions his gentleness, humility and generosity, and underneath that, if not explicitly stated, is an implication of deep sadness. This is unsurprising to anyone who has seen more than one or two of his films. It's all there, underneath the manic tornado of voices and tics, a vast ocean of soulfulness and torment. His characters range from wide-eyed innocents to the weary, wounded and wise, and it is clear that these are all part of the man behind the mask. It's pretty simple psychology to say that the wilder and more insistent the clowning, the deeper the hurt and longing for love, but in this case it seems patently true. Just see the now super-viral joke from *The Watchmen*, about the clown Pagliacci.

Coincidentally, for whatever reason, I put on An *Evening With Robin Williams* last week to listen to in the background while I was cleaning my apartment. I enjoyed all the good-natured Marin-bashing and the old-school early 80s nostalgic vibe and his all-around lovableness, but I couldn't get more than halfway through it. It just became uncomfortable after awhile, this coke-fueled wind-up toy trying so damn hard, so hard you could see the gears turning and popping inside. It definitely had its entertainment value, but a lot of it seemed, not necessarily desperate, but haphazard; as if he were just machine-gunning the audience with gags in hopes that one of the dozen bullets he sprayed out there would hit its mark. One invariably did, but you barely had a moment to laugh before five, six, seven more were on you. His energy was contagious, and he managed to pull you along with his sheer, relentless genius for inhabiting the moment and blowing it out as wide and wild as it would go. It was also fucking exhausting.

It made me wonder if stand-up has changed so much that I've just become accustomed to the subtler rhythms of today's comics, but then I realized, even back then nobody was as manic and off the wall as he was. Even the raging assaults by Sam Kinison and the supercharged impressionistic cavalcades of Richard Pryor and Eddie Murphy stopped to take a breath every once and awhile. His tempo did mellow ever so slightly once he got sober in 1983, and his stand-up got a little bit tighter– I remember his co-hosting of Comic Relief with Whoopi Goldberg and Billy Crystal being particularly funny– but he never lost his incessant ADHD bounce. I've seen dozens of interviewers and talk show hosts try to pin him down and get a word in amidst the whirl of Tasmanian Devil antics. Most of them had little success, but that never seemed to dampen their enjoyment of having him as a guest.

But then off camera, he was famously subdued. His now-legendary conversation with Marc Maron on the WTF podcast is raw and vulnerable and set the precedent for the kind of soul-baring honesty we've come to expect from guests on that show. In addition to musing on comedy, he speaks with generous candor about his struggles with addiction and depression, as well as his heart surgery and marital troubles, and it all takes place in Robin's Tiburon home, the house he died in, which he bought after his divorce, in the same town where he grew up.

Thankfully he found his way to the movies. Or perhaps movies found him. But either way, they offered the Julliard-trained performer the opportunity to inhabit that space where the anarchist wild-child and the brooding empath could not only co-exist, but thrive together on full display. He machine-gunned films the way he machine-gunned jokes. He was relentlessly prolific, sometimes appearing in four or five movies a year. As a result, he made a whole lot of mediocre movies, and even some that are so bad they are considered unwatchable (*Patch Adams, Jack*). Along the way he had plenty of hits, *The Mrs. Doubtfires* and *Aladdins*, and brilliant performances (*The Fisher King, Good Will Hunting*), and some that were both (*Good Morning, Vietnam*). But when he was asked about some of his less-regarded films, he never joined in the bashing. A lot of actors will diplomatically stand up for their own crappy films, defending their choices as well as remaining loyal to the party line. But Robin genuinely appears to have had a place in his heart for all of his films, and had no regrets about any of them. He loved making movies and believed they all have a purpose, however small.

That kind of open-hearted equanimity is admirable and rare, and speaks to the depth of his compassion. I imagine, surely, that part of his prolific output came from a shark-like workaholism— which came from the same place that birthed his mile-a-minute stage persona— the mortal fear of sitting still with oneself too long. But it also came from a puckish fervor for bringing joy to others, a desire to give and to give and then give some more. Because it felt so good to give so much. Also, he loved everything,—slapstick and drama, tragedy and horror, anything that moved and entertained an audience. His range was nearly unmatched. He was known to veer toward the mawkish and sentimental, but he was not afraid of the darkness either. His turns in *Insomnia* and *One Hour Photo* are disturbing and utterly real. These performances were given more power by the actor's lovable persona, the same way that seeing the dad from *Malcolm in the Middle* cooking meth and going up against violent thugs in *Breaking Bad* had a uniquely jarring effect.

In all of this, regardless of what he did, he was beloved. Crappy movie, great movie, funny, dramatic, maudlin, irreverent, it didn't matter. He was universally adored. Because he gave so much of himself. Because he was ridiculously talented. Because he did amazing things. Because he was humble. Because he was kind and thoughtful and always treated people with respect. Because, though it was never explicit, it was clear that something inside was terribly, terribly wounded. You saw it, you felt it, you identified with it. It made the laughter deeper, more meaningful.

Depression, addiction, mental illness, as we well know, are often intimately entwined with creative brilliance. They are not inevitably married to each other, but it stands to reason that the closer we cut to heart of things, the more we let the madness and the poison and the pain flow, the more we let it wash over us, the more we have to live with it, and be burdened by it and somehow try to accept it. Sometimes we are driven to create because it is the only way to salve the wounds of life. It is the only way we can wrest control from the gods, if only fleetingly, if only as part of some self-deceiving illusion. The human soul is remarkable for the extremity of both its resilience and its fragility. It can withstand monumentally inconceivable sorrows and loss; it can be battered beyond recognition and emerge with wisdom and dignity; it is capable of forgiving the unforgivable, facing the most frightening and terrible obstacles, and finding peace and justice in a chaotic, violent and unmerciful cosmos. It can also crumple beneath forces as light as a feather. The simple inevitability of human suffering is universal. We all share the same mortal coil, we weather the same slings and arrows, we struggle to survive, to find love and meaning, protect our children, face old age and decline. Life is a process fraught with hazardous pitfalls, both existential and physical. It's a wonder we make it past as many as we do.

Robin Williams made it past many. He didn't make it past this one. I don't want to get into it here, but fuck those fucking worthless pieces of shit on Fox who like to throw around words like "coward" when it comes to people who commit suicide. No one who makes that decision has any real control at all. They were tossed overboard in the middle of a dark sea, and they treaded water as long as they could, but eventually they couldn't tread anymore. Not because they are weak or selfish or cowardly, but because the human soul, like the human body, has its limits. The human body has only so much blood, so many electrolytes, so many nutrients it can burn through until it expires. The human soul can only take so much hopelessness and pain before its light is extinguished.

It is a terrible fact of depression that it cuts you off from the world. Its goal is to get you alone and destroy you. Robin Williams knew how much he had going for him. He knew how many millions of people loved him, how many great things he had done in his career, that he had been a good and generous person, he'd lived a dynamic, beautiful life, and raised beautiful children, and none of it was enough to save him.

"[T]he human spirit is more powerful than any drug and THAT is what needs to be nourished: with work, play, friendship, family. THESE are the things that matter. This is what we'd forgotten. The simplest things."

Thus says his character at the end of *Awakenings*. Perhaps Robin forgot this himself. Or he became incapable of remembering. Either way, he lost the great battle with the darkness, and as a consequence, we lost one of the true greats.

POST-SCRIPT

The one and only time I met Robin Williams in person, I was a grown man dressed as Harry Potter. It was a highly uncomfortable situation. I was between cafe management jobs, and was filling in the dead air with occasional gigs for a company that booked characters for parties and events. I usually got to wear a full character costume, like a Power Ranger or Sponge Bob, but this one had me feeling pretty awkward. Not only was my costume (despite my seamstress girlfriend's best efforts) completely half-assed and terrible, and my accent inexcusably unconvincing, but I was just way too damn old to be portraying a boy wizard. Nor had I read any of the inane books and I'd only seen one of the movies, so I had very little factual information about the character I was supposed to be embodying. In short, I had absolutely no business being there, but it paid ridiculously well for two hours work, so I decided to surrender my dignity temporarily and do it anyway.

It was a fund-raising auction for some ritzy San Francisco private school, and Ronnie Lott was there, and Peter Coyote, and Robin Williams. I went to his table at some point to talk with the kids there, and while I was humiliating myself by bombarding them with my (probably Australian at this point) accent and garbled Harry Potter knowledge, I looked over and saw him watching me. He smiled and nodded, with that famous twinkle in his eye.

I've always carried that moment with me as a scathing mark on my character, a disapproval from the man on high. I imagined that he saw right through me, immediately sized me up for the pathetic and hapless fraud that I was, and that he knew how little I deserved to be there, "entertaining" his children. Because of course, he was in the top tier of superstar entertainers, and he alone was qualified to dispense all manners of judgment. I know now that most or all of that was just me and my own shit, and it's easy to laugh about it now. I know that if he even acknowledged me at all beyond that fleeting smile, it was an insignificant observation. But nonetheless, at that moment, his gaze had amplified all of the shame and self-loathing I was feeling at the time, and made it impossible to ignore. Under his light I couldn't hide. I was forced to completely inhabit myself.

In hindsight, from what I know about him, I like to think that he was amused by my transparent haplessness; that he pitied me, but also admired the guts it took to make such a plain fool of oneself. I like to think that he saw a bit of himself in me. Not the creative force of nature that imprinted itself so gloriously on our cultural consciousness, but his own vulnerability, his own unsureness about his place in the world, his own guts in facing the confusion and indignities of life. I wish I'd had the wherewithal to say "Hey Robin, guess what? You and I went to the same high school, and at one point they tried to tell me that the most creative and talented person to attend our school was me, not you! What do you think of that?!"

I bet that would have made him laugh.

GRAY

is best known for crumpling up paper into a ball and throwing it behind him. This paper contains words, like a love note, or an apology (or both), the syntax of which he is never be quite satisfied with. He has fallen in love and apologized so many times that the living room and dining room of his apartment have become completely covered with paperballs. He refuses to carry them to the garbage, because he likes to be reminded of failure. There are enough paperballs to completely cover the entire floor of his apartment 5 feet deep. He has a fondness for jumping off of furniture and into the balls, swimming through them from one room to another. This activity reminds him of leaping into leaves in Autumn. Sometimes he writes love letters to the apology letters, and sometimes he writes apology letters to the love letters. Once the collection of paperballs reach the ceiling, Gray will be forced to rent another apartment. He will still he maintain the original apartment with the paperballs. He'll continue returning to it until he can discover the perfect way of saying "I love you, I'm sorry."

Projected Class Schedule

Brian Gray
8/28/09
English 3510

Fall 2003

Rock Climbing – A beginning indoor climbing class focusing on climbing safety, top-rope belaying, bouldering, and beginning climbing technique. No prior roped climbing experience required. Attendance at the first class is mandatory.

US Government and Politics – This is a survey of the institutions and practices of the U.S. government with emphasis placed on political behavior and social conflict. Certain sections taught using service-learning.

Intro to Philosophy – This introductory survey examines the historical development of Western philosophy and philosophical problems concerning truth, reality, & values. The course introduces philosophical methods of inquiry and argumentation. Watch out for the spittle.

Intermediate Algebra – Prereq: Within one year, MATH 0990 with C or better or appropriate CPT or ACT scores. Linear and quadratic equations; inequities; polynominals; rational expressions; radicals; negative and rational exponents; complex numbers; linear systems; introduction to functions; logarithms; and exponential functions. The professor will be from the Czech Republic and very quiet. Furthermore, you hate math. You will get a B-.

Philosophy in Literature – Presents masterpieces of world literature as a narrative means of philosophical problems. Philosophical and literary methodologies are used for analysis of the literary texts. The professor will be a shy and insecure man who nevertheless will introduce you to the books that will change your life.

Spring 2004

Personal Ethics – Exposes students to the essential theoretical frameworks of morality & applies those frameworks to the diversity issues of our times as a systematic means for thinking about moral dilemmas in general & in their own personal lives. You will become a vegetarian as a result of this class and get a tattoo on your left wrist. Again, watch out for his spittle. You will discover a taste for wine when the professor calms you down after an existentialist attack.

Spring 2005

Intro to Film – Introduces students with no previous film training to historical, technical, and aesthetic development of film within its cultural context. Film genres examined. Some materials presented are R-rated. The professor will show his own films, and you will relate to that. You will become more outgoing in this class, but you will still maintain a suspicious distance from social contact.

Quantitative Reasoning – Prereq: MATH 1010 with a C or better or appropriate CPT score. This course focuses on the development of analytical thinking through the application of math to real-life problems. Topics include modeling, logic, financial math, probability, statistics and geometry. Will be taught by a mild-mannered Israeli whose tacky jokes and butterscotch candies will make the incomprehensible subject seem like enchantment. You will decline an invitation.

Computer Essentials – A hands-on introduction to problem solving using Computer tools. Basic hardware and Office software products topics are discussed. Assignments will be typewritten. You will never touch a computer, but a Mormon woman with a husband in Elko will come close to touching you, leaving you to bang your head against a wall.

Political Ideologies – This surveys significant political ideologies, documenting their present and past relevance to society. Emphasis is placed on conservatism, fascism, liberalism, and socialism. Surrounded by conservatives, you will become enraged on a daily basis, but the professor's soothing logic will ease that tension. The final examination will be on the same night of the professor's final examination for his doctorate. When he walks into the room, the class will give him a standing ovation. He will bring the class to their seat and silence with a motion of his hand and inform them that he failed. He will give a lecture about his daughter and "small shiny things." You will take up smoking.

Spring 2006

Human Geography – The thematic study of human activity (population, religion, language, migration, industry) and the global distribution of these activities. This class won't even count towards fucking anything. The teacher will give you Indian khaki, and this will help get through it. You will learn about maps.

Private Guitar – Twelve individual one-half hour guitar lessons. Additional fee is required. This class will fulfill requirements for nothing. The professor, Stan, will teach out of a shed in the back next to his goat pen. You will never figure out why he has goats. Most of what he will teach will be forgotten because you don't really care about classical guitar.

Art History – You know you won't have to take this class but you take it anyway because the drinking will have been getting a little out of control and Jake's back still hasn't healed. You will come to love art and attempt to find a method of living like "Lavender Mist," misconstruing it as a map rather than just a painting. This will lead to an awkward moment at Poor Yorick where $20 and your pants will be stolen. You will consider becoming an art history major.

Intermediate Writing – Prereq: ENGL 1010 with a C or better. Extends the principles of rhetorical awareness and knowledgemaking introduced in English 1010 and increases the ideological engagement within the classroom. Interrogates socioeconomic and political issues. The professor will tell you that "it's a nice travel journal, but not a memoir" and you will look at her with murder in your eyes, and it will send a shiver down her spine.

Critical Intro to Lit – This class will make the magic disappear. The entire class will think you are insane when you burst out into tears repeating "The magic is gone, the magic is gone," several times throughout the semester. They will all think you are wrong, but you prove that you are right. The prosecutor will agree to drop the indecent exposure charge(s) if you agree to plead guilty to the controlled substance charge which is unfair because you hate mescaline and it will all be Rob's idea anyway.

Spring 2007

Intro to Human Anatomy – For non-science majors. Introduction to the human body. The structure, function, and organization of the major organ systems are examined at several levels. This class does not meet the prerequisite requirement of any biology class. The most intriguing part of the class is when the shy professor refers to his wife's clitoris a "fun button." You won't remember anything from this class except for information about the heart.

Earth's Surface Environment – This course examines the interrelationships of land, water, and atmosphere in the human environment. Location of features and countries is also emphasized. The professor will be Wallace Shawn in his role as Vizzini in The Princess Bride. God, you will need a drink. What you learn about tectonic plates will be interesting.

Fall 2007

Intro to Lit Theory – This class won't make sense, but you will fall in love twice, which is appropriate, because that never made sense either. You will develop a relationship with the professor that will increase your skills in ducking behind walls and squirming into crowds whenever you see each other because neither of you will ever learn how to communicate without using the language of garbage trucks hauling ivy mulch to the city dump.

Intro into Romanticism – Despite your disinterest in Romanticism, this class will make the most sense. When the professor describes all of Mary Shelley's miscarriages, you will say "You win some and you lose some" and this is when she has decided that she has had enough or your shit even though there's only two weeks left to the semester. You will ask her out for drinks anyways, and she will decline for personal reasons.

Intro to Modernism – You will take this class, skeptical of the professor before realizing how awful he really is. He will fall to his knees while reading Rimbaud like prayers of a Pentecostal priest. This man's passion is what you have been looking for, which is fortunate, because you will no longer be allowed within 500 feet of any SLCC campus.

Spring 2008

Poetry Workshop – Sitting across from 115 pounds of failure will remind you of that tacky simulacrum of balance you once thought yourself capable of multiplied by 2, and if you don't sway from the booze you will sneak into class, then you'll shake from the anxiety. Fortunately, you will meet someone as unstable as you are with knees twice as wobbly.

Intro to Renaissance Lit – Predictably, there will be jousting tournaments, just not with lances and horses. You will only be able to read the Seamus Heaney translation of Beowulf, and everything else will be in some other language.

Fiction Studies – You will discover your favorite professor. His ambivalence towards life and the university will lead him to change the whole class into autobiography studies despite the title "Studies in Fiction." You let him get away with this because he walks with a burdensome slouch that you will have in about 20 minutes. Studies in autobiography will study a range of authors displaced from their native country. Some are happy about it, and some are upset about it, and some die quiet deaths in the vacuous space of a shotgun barrel. This class will become the professor's own autobiography: disenchantment, yearning, everything except the shotgun barrel.

Fall 2008

Theories of Pop Culture – You will take this class to rehabilitate and restructure relative to the cynicism of magazine ads. Here, you will feel insecure every time you raise your hand, because, let's face it, as much as the man wears cowboy boots you still won't hear what he said, and you still won't have any idea what you are talking about.

Intro to Creative Writing – You will contradict yourself completely by liking it. You will be dismayed to find out that it works.

Reasoning and Rational Decision Making – Analyzing and evaluating arguments, basic logical framework, Aristotelian logic and beginning logic of sentences, fallacies, fundamentals of probability, decision theory, and game theory. Thank you freight trains.

Studies in Modernism – This class will be taught by your favorite professor whose familiar slouch echoes. Again, the course will be changed, this time from "Studies in Modernism" to "Watching Some Birds While Reading a Bunch of Poems." You will swear you can make out a stain of red wine in the professor's beard. He will send you home early several times after looking at the clock and sighing. From this class you will learn the cure for hiccups.

Spring 2009

Survey of Jazz – Survey of Jazz teaches the history and evolution of the art form jazz, and integrates these concepts with cultural, sociological, political, technological, and musical factors. The course exposes students in unique and creative ways to the process in which jazz musicians manipulate musical elements. The professor will be jazz itself, as the lectures will ramble on like a tree branch.

Genre Studies – You will write a short fictional story about a prick and a puddle, and I will call it "The Cactus and the Raincloud," and it will be nonfictional. It will be both fictional and nonfictional because (1) it is true, but (2) so unreal. You will acquire 257 umbrellas.

Form and Theory – That 115 pound failure will force you to withdraw from this class because you will no longer think it is appropriate to drink in class anymore, so it's either the booze or you and you choose you. This course description is included is because of the insidious "W" forever embroidered upon your transcript.

Studies in 20th Century American Literature – You will cringe at the professor's misinterpretation of Walter Benjamin's "Art in the Age of Mechanical Reproduction" for about half of the semester, because what most people don't realize is the historical context in which it was written, thereby rendering the piece a glorification of mechanical reproduction rather than a lament of it. You will later cringe at the fact that you cringed in the first place and take 7 shots of gin to recover from so much cringing.

<u>Summer 2009</u>

Theories of Gender/Sexuality in International Literature – Somehow you will manage to maintain sobriety, and even quit smoking. For a second you will hold a moment of comprehensibility before you, as if suspended right before your eyes, but when you reach for it you will be forced to apologize repeatedly to the professor, who will apologize in return.

The Global Citizen – This course will serve as a guide for international travelers and those desiring a career in the global marketplace. Students will learn to make responsible choices when planning and engaging in travel experiences regardless of the purpose of the international trip. Exactly.

<u>Fall 2009</u>

Studies in Narrative – This class will explore the post-modern novel, and. And. End. Maybe. 4'33" Considerable clouds early. Some decrease in clouds later in the day. I'm the first in line to offer organizational criticism and offer my apologies to the victim and accept responsibility for having missed an earlier opportunity to extend the previous session's positive bias into after-hours trading by posting a better-than-expected adjusted $0.28 per share for its latest quarter.

Writing Fiction – You will think you know how to handle this class because you know how to type words on a computer, like these words, but apparently you will need more than that. At times you will wonder if you are too far gone to theory, like a surgical patient with too much blood loss, to ever allow the imagination to traipse down dark, suspicious alleyways where anything could happen. At one point you will actually walk down a dark, suspicious alleyway hoping something will happen and be worth writing about, but nothing happens, so you will go into the bar at the end of the alleyway, learn how to line dance, puke twice on the floor, and attain countless numbers of gay men you will never intend on calling. One of them will be named Richard. Drunkenly, you will stumble home, and in the middle of the well-lit street, right outside of your doorway, your neighbor will take your wallet. He won't so much take it, but, rather, you will give it to him. Then you will go inside, write four words across a blank page, and ask for your wallet back in the morning.

Form and Theory – You will give this class another shot, because you are familiar with the professor. Instead of syllables, the professor will count letters. This will seem more appropriate, calming, transfixing, barbiturate. You will spend most of the class with your eyes transfixed to a spot of blue on a green wall that probably isn't there. Your mouth will move, but you won't hear the words that come out of them, they will just come out, like prisoners escaping a maximum-security prison. You will begin suspect that the professor does not have nipples, no matter how great his poetry is. Eventually, you will amass hundreds of receipts, all of them rhyming.

Theories of Culture – This class will be boring boring boring. The voice of the professor will be soothing white noise, perfect conditions for falling peacefully into a deep slumber each class, sometimes lasting hours after class, when it is dark outside and you are all alone with fine strings of saliva trailing from your mouth onto the desk. It will not help to get inebriated before class. You will consider dropping it, but opt to fail it just to make a point. At the last minute, you will get the professor drunk and get him to think you are a pretty nice guy. He will give a C+ and you will give him a hand job.

Intermediate French 1 – Third-semester French. Continued emphasis on listening and speaking skills with an increased emphasis on reading and writing skills through the study of short selections of French literature. The professor will make sense even if the words do not. You'll form a bond over a cigarette, and fail every test for the rest of the semester. You'll never learn French, but she will seem perplexed at the meaning of letters in the American university system, and you will pass. She will flee to Andorra, claiming it was your fault.

Spring 2010

Writing Poetry – You will give in with full submission. You will not be sure if it works or if it is effective until 14 years later, but even that won't be enough proof.

Intermediate French 2 – Fourth-semester French. This course maintains a strong emphasis on listening and speaking skills. Through readings of more extensive texts and informal writing as a support for speaking, it develops oral fluency toward narration/ elaboration and paragraph-length discourse. You won't understand a word of it. You will go to all of your professor's barbecues, even in the middle of winter, when you swear to god he has lost his mind. You will even go as far as to answer his phone calls at 1:24 in the morning, drive down to South Salt Lake with a single gallon of gasoline, meet him in a sketchy part of town asking "What are you doing in this part of town," and he will respond simply, "Vous ne voulez pas savoir," and drive away, hitting a mailbox and a cat. The distance in his eyes will be comforting for some reason.

Non-major Painting – This is a fundamental course in painting that will provide instruction in basic techniques to beginners. Concepts of shape, volume, and color theory are emphasized. Instructors will teach indirect painting (glazes) and direct painting. Some concentrate on representation and others treat the class as a free-form experience. Non-art major class. It will be different from an English class. You will instantly fall in love with it, despite the awful products of your efforts, and your over-use of the colors "orchid," and "teal." Somehow your girlfriend will continue to love you despite the odd collages of color that will inhabit every corner of the apartment.

Advanced Seminar British Studies – Your favorite professor will teach this course. His approach will be more rigorous than previous courses. His demeanor will seem more cheerful, though the selections will not be. The suspicion of the wine stains streaking his beard will be confirmed. The obsession with Virginia Woolf will persist, and he will give a wicked simper when he assigns Ulysses. You will not read it. You will have given up on reading long ago. Letters won't seem to come together anymore, and all you will want is more and more orchid and more and more teal. On the last day of class, you will accompany him in his stroll out to the lawn outside the ugly post-war building. You will lie down in it, leaning and loafing at ease. He will take out a bottle of port from his bag and offer it to you. You will take it, and take copious swigs. The sun will go down, it will be Spring. Not a word will be said until you feel the first gulp begin to grip your stomach and strangle your sobriety. He will say, "Look, the birds in the trees." You will say, "Yes. Great. Robins. I think." And he will say, "Actually, I think, they're sand cranes." You will know this is not true because at that point neither of you will be able to see that far, but you will say, "It's singing, like a robin." And he will say, "Yes. Should snow tomorrow." And you will say, "That's terrible. For them. They're singing. Too early." And he will say "It's Spring. It came too soon."

Question Mark

I have been trying
to unbend all of my question marks
so they will resemble exclamation points,
and there will be no more uncertainty,
only excitement.
Now,
there's no longer a need
for answers.
Just celebration.

My palms have become blistered,
my fingertips callused
from attempting
to place the paper fibers
into a more satisfying alignment.
All of my questions
have now become awkward exclamations,
such as
"Who do you think you are!"
"What is the meaning of life!"
"You're pregnant!"

I am also trying to straighten out
other bends in my life.

If I could straighten out
my last lover's hips,
then I could actually become excited
about the prospect of making love
rather than feeling
a despondence
a deep existential doubt about
our relationship,
how this is what we do instead of talk,
how this is quite possibly
the last time
we will ever make love again.

If I could straighten out
my 92-year-old grandmother's back,
then she could live

the remainder of her life
in joy and exuberance
rather than taking small, careful steps
through her living room,
her spine
punctuating every single
Alzheimer's statement
about who and where she is,
forced to gaze at the floor
as though searching for
tiny fragments of her life
that broke away and dissolved
into the worn fibers
of the carpet.

Finally,
I could straighten out
that drunken 80 mph bend
in the road
coming down the canyon
during that stupid winter,
then you would still be here
with me tonight
and we could still go
shot-for-shot
still
yell
obscenities
at each
other
from
across the room,
still
dancing
and dancing
and dancing,
and dancing
like idiots,
like death
isn't lingering
with his
inquisitive breath
on our
shoulders,

Instead I sit here alone, in this room, drinking by myself, staring at the wall, attempting to push paper fibers into alignment, asking your ghost "What the hell were you thinking?"

ROBERT
DUNCAN GRAY

aka COLDGOLD is a charming shitlord artist currently living in Portland, OR. He is the author of IMMACULATE / THE RHODODENDRON AND CAMELLIA YEAR BOOK (1966) (University of Hell Press) and a pioneer of transcendental R&B noise.

To Unfuck It All

I unwrap a package That
Doesn't have my name on it
To find inside A severed head
Now I need a poem To raise the dead
I'd like One day To open a menu
And order A Poem That might compel
A Reader To walk beside A body
Of water Not thinking corpse

I need a poem To bury
in a small box But I disgust
myself With bleeding words
As lifeless flesh cooling Once
And then warming again
In the sun On the concrete
Carrion song

Look at the dead thing
But don't touch it Look at birds
How do you write about
Dead bodies? How do you Not
Write about dead bodies?
Each morning I dig
A small grave with my
Naked hands It's cold

For the love of everything
That is fucked
A poem
To unfuck
It all
Is not a poem
No Blood on the surface
Of the Moon

Now be a dead friend
And play
Horses again
Now be a dead friend
And play again
Horses

Haggard Europe and the Graveyard of Human Rights

Would you like
To love each other

In traffic perhaps Never
having had a brother

To leave in the car
Or lose at the Supermarket

It's different
In different places

But small birds
Mostly the same

I kiss Death
On damp forehead

Like a mauve child
And Breathe easy

Do a good thing
On a slow day Observe

How drunk you are
In the garden

As I look out
The kitchen window

Pigeons with teal
And pink neck soft

Shimmy in dumb sun
Bobbing small heads

I Water dead vegetables
Make them alive

Weekend brings

Dried Persimmon and Death

I have been
Paper toweled

Lindsay is sewing soft fruit
On Saturday night Right

There's blood in the sink
But it Looks like Flowers to me

Distraction Can Be Deadly

I wouldn't eat
Your asshole I said

If I didn't
Like the taste

I never remember
How to pronounce I said

Peonies
Honey in the Hallway I said

The humanity of animals I said
Where does your mind go

During a seizure
Because I don't want

To get in trouble
With the devil I said

Amelia
Getting her last good

Haircut I said
You are beautiful

I noticed your legs
And died I said

And that was
The truth at the time

HEATHER A

Heather's stories feature a self-obsessed train wreck alcoholic named Haley. DIS-CLAIMER: In real life, Heather is nothing like Haley. Heather is a warm hearted person. You'd have no problem introducing Heather to your grandmother or asking her to babysit your kids. (Especially if your kids are boys, between the ages of 18 to 20.)

NOBODY DIES ALONE - Ask Heather A #4 - It Buuuurn!

dear heather,

so i did something i wouldn't normally do and i went home with this guy from a bar the other night. i was really drunk and i slept with him of course. i dont remember it well enough to know if it was even good or not but that's not the problem. i woke up the next morning and it was awkward and i left without really saying goodbye he was in the bathroom and i just said goodbye though the door. when i got home i realized that all the money from my wallet was gone and i think i had at least 70 or 80 dollars in there. theres a small chance that i spent it or lost it and don't remember but i dont really think so. what if he stole it? what do i do? i dont really want to see him again or talk to him, and i dont know how i'd get him to admit it anyway. but i just want to know what happened. that kind of money is a lot to me these days. who would do that kind of thing anyway? please help.

mary s

oakland, ca

Dear Mary,

I just read your letter and became outraged. But don't worry, as a professional MENSA dating advice genius I channeled my rage into PURE STRATEGY.

Most advice columnists would tell you to track this fucker down and pull ye olde timey favorite: "Hi, I'll need some money for an abortion, please." But ye olde abortion trick is so 2014. I've got something new for you – you'll get $750 for this one, which makes up for your time, effort, and emotional investment. But, what's absolutely priceless? TEACHING THIS FUCKER A LESSON.

First, you're going to need to show up at his place of business. Yes, find out where he works. (If he's jobless, find the bar he hangs out, the pinball machine he lords over, or anywhere he has a "reputation" to uphold.) You are going to have to approach him, off guard at work, in public, in front of people. But here's the thing: 1) You aren't going to act like yourself and 2) You are going to speak in what I like to call a "handicapped voice." You know what I am talking about. If not, the handicapped voice may come naturally to you.

Once you see this guy, use the "handicapped voice" and VERY SLOWLY but in a SUPER LOUD HC VOICE say the following: "It burns. It burns. You put your pee-pee inside me and now I burn down there." Then, I want you to open the elastic waistband of your pants, look down, and point to your crotch. Keep it simple. Look back up at him, but keep holding your waistband open. Repeat: "It burns. It burns."

You'll need a few props. I've already mentioned the elastic-waist pants. You'll also need to wear a big diaper, so people can see it. You'll also need a walker. If you don't have a walker, I recommend an eye patch, a box of Entenmann's donuts, or a half melted popsicle (either blue or red.) If you use the donuts, make sure that chocolate and powdered sugar are all over your face. If you go with the popsicle, make sure it melts all over your hand and falls on the ground while you're talking.

This fucker is going to jump to action. But, be warned: he might deny knowing you.

STAY STRONG. If he starts saying that you're a crazy liar, I want you to GO RAIN-MAN and repeat his home address. Repeat it over and over. And then: "It burns. It burns when I pee-pee." He'll usher you away from the fray and demand to know what's going on. That's when you very quietly demand that he give you 600 – 800 dollars. Tell him he stole your money and this is the tip of the iceberg. Tell him that you are just getting started. You are going to make his life a living hell.

If this guy is a hard core sociopath and doesn't immediately acquiesce – start drooling. If he doesn't pull out his wallet in 15 seconds, start to hop around and grab your crotch and talk about the burning. Maybe say: "You gonna put it inside me again? Like last time? It so small but it's hurt when I pee pee. It BURRRRRRRRRN."

Maybe right now your conscious is screaming out : *NO, I can't do that. That sounds humiliating. I'm not that kind of person!!!* Mary, ask yourself: What kind of asshole steals money from a drunk girls wallet? This is justice, okay? Don't do it for yourself. Do it for humanity. Retribution is a mother fucker.

And I know that there are people who think it's offensive that I'm telling you to ACT developmentally disabled. In my defense, I have nothing but respect for developmentally disabled folks. In fact, judging from the Facebook status updates alone, I'd estimate that about 30% of my friends are developmentally disabled. AND, last but not least, there was a time in my life when I, Heather A Dating Advice Genius Tripple MENSA, was considered MENTALLY DISABLED, okay?

Anyway …. Watch *What's Eating Gilbert Grape* and channel your inner Leonardo DiCaprio. Tune in your inner Dustin Hoffman, a la Rainman. You're a loveable mentally retarded girl, with a melted popsicle, and a diaper. It buuuuuuuurns. You've got absolutely nothing to lose. Now make this fucker regret the day he was born. I know you can do it.

And remember, as you eat the last of those powdered donuts and stack those dollah-dollah bills, Nobody Dies Alone.

Heather A.

NOBODY DIES ALONE - Ask Heather A # 6: True Love Quiz

H-
What is the definition of true love?
B
Grand Rapids, MI

Dear B,

That is a magical question. Some idiots say that love is intangible That it can't be defined or quantified. Lucky for you, I'm a Professional Dating Advice Triple MENSA Genius, and I've developed a test that gives you a definitive number on where you stand re: your feelings for that SPECIAL SOMEONE.

GOOD LUCK,

Heather A.

You've cried over your Special Someone (+1 point)

at least three times (+5 points)

you've cried at least three times, hung up on the phone at least twice, and broken up at least three times (+10 points)

you've also screamed "It's fucking over, I mean it this time. God as my fucking witness." (+15 points)

and then you've driven over to his house, two hours later. (+30 points)

You've torched some of your Special Someone's possessions (+25 points)

You've driven by their house, in secret (+1 point)

It's no secret! (+ 10 points)

You've parked in front of his house, watching his silhouette for at least an hour (+10 points)

for two hours (+15 points)

a few days (+25 points)

When you think about being away from your Special Someone you ...

feel like throwing up (+ 1 point)

throw up (+3 points)

you consider taking a swan dive off a tall building (+ 1 point)

you're on the ledge right now (+100 points)

All of the above. (FUCK IT. YOU CAN STOP TAKING THE TEST RIGHT NOW, BECAUSE THIS IS TRUE LOVE. IT DOESN'T GET BETTER THAN THIS.)

You've considered taking a welding class …

so that you can brand yourself with the special someone's initials (+ 15 points)

and then … take picture of it, so you can post that shit on Facebook (+ 10 points)

and tag your special someone (+ 20 points)

You have the baby photos of your Special Someone, hidden in your phone. (+1 point)

You have the baby photos of your Special Someone, NOT hidden in your phone. (+ 5 points)

Speaking of phones, you have one of those tracking devices in your phone so that you can easily find your Special Someone, no matter where they are. (+1 point. Everyone does this shit, apparently.)

You tell people that the tracking phone app is ONLY FOR ERRANDS. Example: "If my Special Someone is near a pet store, I can tell him that kitty might need cat food." (+ 2 points. You're a liar.)

You don't lie about why you have the app. You say: "Yeah, I'm straight up clocking that motherfucker. If he goes within a mile of that skank's house, I WANT TO KNOW." (+10 points)

You agree to watch a three hour long documentary on Siberian Trappers, because your Spec. Someone says "I heard this was supposed to be good." (+ 5 points)

When your Special Someone suggests going out for Buffalo Wild Wings and watching a sporting event with his college friends, you say: "OH MY GOD. That sounds amazing." (+10 points)

Those friends wear visors and can't remember your name. (+5 points)

You're a vegetarian. (-10 points. I have my reasons. Mainly: vegetarians don't deserve love.)

————

50 points or less – your heart is a black-hole vortex of ice

100 – 125 points – try harder. Maybe an isolation tank 3 + weeks.

125 – 175 points – warmer.

175 – 300 points – ballpark.

300 + points – Jackpot!!! Please email us at mailbox@drunkinamidnightchoir. com for your Nobody Dies Alone T-Shirt.

M.E. HIRSH

M. E. Hirsh lives, works and plays (and drinks ridiculous amounts of earl grey) in the Shire. She likes to take pictures with her phone.

JOANNA HOFFMAN

   is a poet and teaching artist living in Brooklyn, New York. Her full-length book of poetry, Running for Trap Doors (Sibling Rivalry Press) was nominated for a Lambda Literary Award and featured in the American Library Association's list of recommended LGBT reading for 2013. When not performing poems, Joanna works at a nonprofit, bikes around Brooklyn and tries to convince her cat to wear bow ties.

What I Love About What I'll Never Understand

I used to think I'd get over a heartbreak faster
if I could understand where it all went wrong.
If love is forever, and she says she stopped
loving me, then it must never have been love.
There—a neatly wrapped devastation, stitches
glittering gold. I felt the same way about death
at 16 when my aunt died of cancer. Energy is
immortal, so she's still here somewhere, so
there's less absence to mourn. Except that
I still couldn't see her, or hug her, ever again.
So science, too, is a blind devotion to faith
for everyone except the scientist. I love to
Google everything, but I also love that there
are some things Google can never tell me
or, at least, can never provide an answer
that satisfies me, like "Why do people become
serial killers?" or "Does my cat love me?" or
"Will there ever be a cure for cancer?" I read
today that scientists are learning to remove
HIV from cells, or make them more responsive
to chemotherapy, or even to play god for
parents with conditional love for their
someday babies. I love knowing that there
is so much I will never understand how
to do, like isolate a gene or sculpt a statue
or fall in love with a man or know if cancer
is my destiny. There's a kind of peace in
admitting what is beyond me. I am fluent
in failures and sometimes success. In
enough self-doubt for a galaxy of galaxies.
I don't ever want it all to make sense. If
science is a faith, then discovery is prayer.
Look—a vaccine for cervical cancer. An
end to HIV. Eyes wide with awe and
humility. A bush on fire. A promise that
I'll never really be alone.

I Don't Want to Disappear

This Ambien is a voluntary eclipse;
the softest exit from the rusted belly
of a dead, floating whale. I grew up
believing Care Bears were furry little
Gods—when they watered the clouds,
it rained. When they bowled, thunder.
And O, how the Care Bear Stare made
my own belly shine every time I wished
a motherfucker would. Tenderheart
Bear, I hope I dream of you, you
benevolent little marshall of the sky.
Please float me home. Please don't
let me disappear. Don't let fear be
the anthem of my beginning and my
end. Please God. Please TenderHeart Bear.
Please Cheer Bear and FunShine Bear.
Whoever and whatever you are. Please God
that I am to myself. Please pull the strings.
Please save a life. Please let the landing
be so soft, I wake up already
on the ground.

Wilderness Tips

Praise the stupid, broken heart that still
bends its animal ears towards her footsteps.
This is how hope out-Houdini's the straitjacket;
how the half-eaten deer coaxes the tiger
to open her jaw. I can't blame the wilderness
for being wild. You can buy insurance
for Kim Kardashian's thumbnail but not
for the human heart. When I throw up
my hands it's the kind of fuck this
that pulls the laughter from my reluctant gut.
I didn't plan this party. I don't even work here.
When I say my heart is broken I mean that
I haven't felt anything since the day I realized
she wasn't going to ask me to take her back.
Just snap, then cold static, then air. This is
how the snake swallows its own tail; how
numbness is a cast mummifying my fear;
how fear is a cast mummifying my anger.
I am terrified of anger. I don't know how
to be angry without collapsing in apologies.
Praise the stupid, broken girl that still
bends her animal knees towards what made her.
This is how loss hollows out a new room
to be lived in. I want to believe I still live
in this body, but I haven't felt myself for months.
Praise the waning summer, how time yanks
the snake forward by the throat and the skin
left behind is a necessary sacrifice. It's not
mean to survive. Praise the body that knows
what it does and doesn't want, how this
is the only survival I had to barter for,
how I guard it with my teeth.

JELAL HUYLER

Jelal is a man who likes hats
and wears many of them
one of his favorites is the WriterHat

and so he writes things...

He lives inside a sprawling never-ending sentence and hopes with all his heart that he
will someday be able to translate the experience into something the outside world can
commune with.

Also he really reeeeally likes hats.

p.s.
you can buy a wee little book of his poetry, at this address:

http://thegorillapress.com/authors/yjelalhuyler/

Hashtag

No one here moves
but everyone has got real good at not moving

The dust mites think we are mentally disabled
they thank dust mite god for this fact

We poop in circles
and no one feels ashamed because no one ever actually
looks up from their lap
toilet paper and silence and no one
remembers what laughing aloud feels like

The feelings drown themselves with our hands
and call it update
our fingers no longer possess the need for other fingers
we have other things to finger now
more important thingers now
to finger now
to thing or
how
you
figure?

There are still pets sometimes
though it's the wall which feeds and waters them
and our fingers are mostly occupied with not flesh
the pets still seek to us sometimes and sniff
our horribly circulating toes
and nuzzle forearms
and wait for our deaths

Death still comes too
but he's older
most of us think he's kind of out of date
not that we can ignore him
just he's not the topic he once was
just overdone, you know?
like you see anyone's face enough times
and you get kind of bored with it

Sex is gone.

But there is food still
we eat it a lot or a little or almost not at all
and it is tasteless
no matter what the flavor

There is music
but we've mostly lost our ears
we recognize it mostly only as a thing that reminds
us of what we imagine
sex must have felt like.
none of us know,
but good right?
it must have been good.

Excitement is hard to come by
but you can get some still if you got the cash
an you're really serious about it

There is no cash anymore
just bitworth, everyone has the standard amount allotted at birth (which is minuscule)
plus whatever their parents are or were able to add (which varies from minuscule to
disproportionate)
but there is less crime
or at least we don't get much crime reported to us
or very much of anything reported to us for that matter
or very much of anything

But there is time
lots of time
lots and lots of time
lots and lots and lots and lots and
people buy lots of time
and build spaces over those lots
and live in those spaces
and get even more good at not moving because
there is time
there is always time

So

Things haven't changed much
except none of us remember what things were like before
but

things are good now
or
things are
now
at least
we think they are

There are still faces
we don't really see much of them any longer
but we know they are there
and we still talk to each other
kind of
we kind of still
do

BUT
There is much information to be had
and connection speeds improve every day
and we can reach anywhere any time any place in less than seconds and we can learn
anything out there that is out there
we can have it
any of it
all of it
a lot or a little
and really who would trade that for anything
except maybe

to know what sex felt like

good right?

it must have been good.

The Fox News Building is Literally a White Portico'd Slave Mansion House... Look It Up

the sky is darkening but the blue is still magnificent
and there is a crinkling mass of wrinkleflesh giblet-lipped hungering
behind my left ear
it wants to speak with me
share me its opinion
i do not want its opinion
but i listen anyway
the news is all falsified
the window wipers wash nothing
but make smudge
and the cigarette is leaning out the window
throwing dirty looks at passerby

the window is stuck open
not far
and the greasing
is as that of gravy filled glass tray
having sat crusting for some time
and still the incessant whisperdroning of that same
monotonous song

<death murder="" death="">
</ death>
dick murder pussy
money pussy greed
greed pussy tragedy
tragic butis life>

crinkling mass of wrinkleflesh thinks its funny

i think i have gone insane.

Untitled Wariable z

and so then
a flower bloomed
and the boy picked it
and it was him
and this was good
so the boy smiled
but he'd picked it
so he cried too

WILLIAM JAMES

is a poet, punk rocker, & train enthusiast who recently appeared in the *Ask Trains Q&A* column of TRAINS Magazine. He is the author of *rebel hearts & restless ghosts* (Timber Mouse Publishing, 2015). He currently lives in Manchester, NH, where he pretends to be older & more curmudgeonly than he really is.

After 18 Months The
Sentence Is Commuted

August.
Grace is crying and bleeding in my backseat, spilling
sadness on the upholstery like copper & ink. Years later
in a poetry workshop, I will attempt to *write about the stain
that will never come out* & this memory will haunt me
like a stubborn ghost.

November.
I read that rabbits have to constantly chew
to file down their teeth or else sharp enamel
will erupt from their lips, splitting the flesh
beyond repair. Overcome with my own need
to chew, I pinch my most sacred sharp thing
between my fingers & turn out the lights.
Let the dark swallow me. Welcome the embrace
of the knife.

September.
I learn that terrorists have taken over a plane
with nothing more than boxcutters, sending
hundreds of passengers hurling to their death.
I look at my left forearm, wracked with guilt.

December.
Dripping wet scarlet, staining the tile
on the floor of the communal dorm shower.
A paper sign hung above the mirror reads
*You are an adult. The housekeeping staff is not
your mother. Please clean up after yourself.*

December.
In the campus health center, I am a paper tab printed
with a number. An unwanted customer in a hostile butchery.
A voice calls to the counter me but does not bother
taking my name. I am told there is nothing wrong with me
except sin. Except disgrace. A nurse hands me a pamphlet

titled *God's Answers To Our Deep Hurts,* says she'll leave me
alone to pray.

December.
I have not left my room in seventeen days.
A letter from my adviser slips under my door,
informing me that due to my plummeting GPA
I am no longer welcome at this institution.
The letterhead chronicling my failure reads
Rigorously Academic. Unapologetically Christian.

December.
Half-past midnight. The stroke of cliché. I am standing
next to the railroad tracks that divide the campus, shadowed
on the south end. A long freight train passes
like a slow moan, like a wounded animal howling.
I want to jump. To be swept to my reward by coal dust.
Instead of dying, I open my throat, screaming against the roar.

January.
The bedroom in my parents house is the same
as when I left it behind. Black paint covering
the walls, the window blocked by cheap plywood.
No light can touch me. I am safe here.

February.
The doctor in the sweater vest does not look up
from his notepad once during our session. I tell him
everything I can remember. He hands me a prescription,
says *take one of these twice a day for the next six months.*
He does not look me in the eye. He does not speak my name.

February.
My caseworker's name is Gale—spelled like the storm. She has seen
every terrible thing humanity has to offer, and reminds me of this
with every session. Gale says I just need to have some perspective.
Says *just keep taking your meds as prescribed, things will look up.*
She does not look me in the eye. She does not speak my name.

February.
In the shower at my parents house,
& my skin will not come clean. I scrub
hard enough to scab, but the self-pity
sticks to me like tar. I swing my fist
full of hate & thin steel. Suddenly
the bathtub is full of blood.

February.
Gale meets me in the ER. Gives a knowing glance
at the new sutures. Her voice, a storm layered in disgust
& disappointment says *I could have you committed
for this, but we both know that won't do any good.
We both know you don't* want *to get better.*

February.
Hospital. Overdose. The doctor who won't look me in the eye
stands me in line for medication with everyone else on the ward.

He tells me *I'm increasing your dosage*
& February is a fog I can only sleep through.

March.
My coworkers on the grocery store night shift
whisper to each other in speculation. Every time
I open a new box, they look suspiciously
at the boxcutter in my hand, waiting for the serpent to strike.

April.
My mother bleaches the porcelain tub. Buys new bath towels,
dark enough not to stain. She tells me she will always love me
no matter what. I want to tell her I'm sorry, but all I can whisper is
I know.

June.
My new county caseworker's name is Ray. When I meet him
for the first time, Ray is wearing a Harley-Davidson t-shirt
under a leather vest. He tells me *all of my training expects me*

to put people into nice, neat little categories. But people aren't neat.
They're messy and disorganized, and nobody fits in a textbook-shaped box.

July.
I see Ray for the 2nd to last time. He tells me *never forget,*
you're more than your diagnosis, more than your disorder.
He doesn't ask me any probing questions or offer any cliches.
Says *wherever you go with your writing, whenever you make it big,*
remember who got you there. And maybe remember me as well.
It takes me years to realize he offered these as separate things.

August.
I see Ray for the last time. He wishes me well,
tells me *you're gonna be just fine, and one day*
you can use this experience to relate to someone
who needs to know they're not alone.
He shakes my hand, looks me in the eye,
says his goodbyes addressing me by name.

Strange Language

after Sean Patrick Mulroy

The first time your father curses God, you are
three years old. There is a photograph of you – innocent,
naked, or wrapped in diapers. You don't remember which
but you know that you were screaming. Fist clenched,
mouth agape as though your lungs alone could
shout down Jericho's walls. Your mother has told you
this story many times. She tells you how you always were
just like him. How even at a young age you would
imitate every motion, every muscle twitch. How
your eyes were tiny mirrors.

The first time your father curses God, you are
too young to realize what sounds are taking shape
in his mouth. You have not yet learned the meaning of
words like *depression, mood disorder, mentally ill* . You know
sickness as the way your belly cries itself empty, know pain as
stepping on an alphabet block or the neighbor's dog
nipping at your fingers. You know that sometimes,
Daddy turns monster. Yells strange language. You know
sometimes your mother cries quiet into breakfast
when she thinks you are not paying attention.

You do not know why this is sadness, just that it is.

You practice imitation for years. Learn his mannerisms. Learn
the meaning of words like *legacy, bloodline, only son*. You
remember your sister, half-drowned in the bathtub. How her hair
floated peacefully, how her head bobbed under the water
held by a sleepy rage. You learn how to turn your viper's
inheritance backwards. Point shotguns at your own mouth instead.
Dig into your skin trying to prune your family tree.
Your mother does not stop crying, but she hides it less often.

The first time your father curses God, your mouth
is a slow-speed car crash wrapped around his oaths. He
takes your tiny fists into his palms. Bends your arms backwards,
peels you wishbone crooked. Looks into your tiny mirror eyes,
says *little one, repeat after me. Say it.*
Say it just like this.

93

Screaming Thunderbox
(Obsolete Engine Blues)

for the EMD F40PH

Hallelujah for the hard edges, angles
        sharp & raw, how they slice the wind
               in ribbons of red & white, carving
the landscape in slipstream swathes.

Hallelujah for the blood-nose
        patina of rust charging valiant
               into dark tunnels, spaghetti strands
of rail, from Union to Penn & back.

Hallelujah for the soot-black, thick
        diesel smoke chuff-chuff-chuffing
into air, spewing clouds of dark fog

        like foam flecking at the mouth,
three-thousand horses lunging
        against the weight of the consist, hallelujah

for the consist; for the diner
        with its too-strong coffee & stale
               baked goods, the coach rattling
like unsettled bones,

hallelujah for the glass dome
        of the lounge, how it opens our eyes
               to the gates of heaven, all the stars
of the sky in their brilliant hues,

a still-life of snow caps, glacial streams,
        tumbleweed & fields of wheat royal
               as the finest throne room, this majesty
the highways keep locked away from us.

Give praise to the fury in its belly,
        to the horn ringing out a muted coronation
               song, give praise & sing hallelujah
to the dulcet chorus of the bell,

how its gentle nudge guides us
to the safety of distance, calling us
like children to the comfort of home.

ROBERT LASHLEY

is a literary bluesologist, an up south soul brother, and a homeboy who likes to let his bookishness speak on the page. His full length book: The Homeboy Songs, was published by Small Doggies press in April 2014. Like his hero, James Baldwin, he wants to be an honest man and a good writer.

L. L, April 7, 3:17pm

(Or when the doctor asked why the homeboy
stabbed himself, he responded in stanzas)

Someday, my blood will never be a sunset.
Someday, my brain will not be used up .
Someday, I'll wake and know where the time went .

"The needle took her", the text message sent
then I took my scissors and drinking cup.
Someday, my blood will never be a sunset.

Away from this world, her needle bent .
Away from life, I left, in sip by sip.
Someday, I'll wake and know where the time went.

I wanted to go. But what I meant
I wanted to see her in one last trip.
Someday, my blood will never be a sunset.

Without her, everyday is lent,
everyday away from her arms and lips.
Someday, I'll wake and know where the time went.

In the wilderness I live-write-repent-
In wilderness away from death's sharp tip.
Someday, my blood will never be a sunset.
Someday, I'll wake and know where the time went.

When God Lets My Body Be

*(After the E. E Cummings Poem
Of The Same Name)*

When god lets my body be
from each ripped wound shall sprout a tree
of fruit that exists only for you .

My rosary beads will make you a laurel
of crowns, medallions
and alleyway garlands
no one but us can see.
My love, let me be your unknown color.
Let my back beget an afro sun
that turns inner deaths asunder.
That recolors all my ordinary worlds
into beauty from scabs of black
(that hold poisoned rivers).
Then, my love, I will swim into hell
and part out it's ashen seas.

Love, our legs are a nation of labyrinths.
I want to wander with you
with no thought to go home
and no law greater than your conceit.
My riddles and scars
I will lay at your feet
and alchemize into acres of orchids.

How Not to Think About Slavery
While Listening to Three 6 Mafia

(Or, No, I Don't Think It's That
Hard Out Here for a Pimp)

Look away from their ice, the glitter and such.
Do not think of cattle, oxen, or pain
for their pictures, though silent, say far too much.

Don't think of their blood, the soul catcher's punch,
the taking of bounty with encrusted chain.
Look away from the ice, the glitter and such.

Don't think of the gentry, the dawg's or the Dutch
nor the color of their dirt, their clay or their grain
for their pictures, though silent, say far too much.

Don't think of their auction, their prod or their touch
their sizing of the breast, testicles, brain.
Look away from the ice, the glitter and such.

Don't think of the bee, the chopping block crutch
and the cut of the day, come shine or come rain
for their pictures, though silent, say far too much.

To think of it all is to think far too much.
To think far too much is to think you're insane.
Look away from their ice, the glitter and such
for their pictures, though silent, say far too much.

CHILLBEAR LATRIGUE

Chillbear Latrigue is the pen name of Michael Davis, a founding contributor and editor at *Drunk in a Midnight Choir*. When not aggressively toiling to make raw, honest poetry and literature more accessible to the literate masses, he dabbles in fighting crime as an American law enforcement officer (working well within the established constitutional parameters of his profession). Chillbear hangs his hat in a small burg in Broward County, Florida, but he hates it there.

The Highly Imposing Man's Guide to Surviving Breakups With Dignity

We used to have the French Foreign Legion. It was a group of men you could join with the confidence that comes from knowing that there wasn't going to be a lot of talk about feelings. You could hunker down in your foxhole with your bayonet and ammo pouch, eating cheese, sipping low-grade brandy from a flask, knowing that sooner or later a ball from the enemy's rifle would kill that thing that was gnawing away at your gut—along with the rest of you. Maybe, during the armistice, while the guns were cooling, to the sympathetic ears of your brothers in arms, you would quietly utter the four words—and only those four words—that would explain what the fuck you were doing in the middle of the goddamn Sahara killing Saracens: "because of a woman."

Amour rejeté. Rejected love.

Those were simpler times, and the political wind has shifted. While it's no longer considered heroic to subjugate a less developed civilization just because your heart hurts, the suffering you're feeling is too profound to idly sit by, waiting for it to heal. You're numb; you're in pain; and you're drifting with a humiliating lack of direction. Well, I have news for you, frenchy: no one gives a damn. Not your family. Not your friends. Least of all her. If you're looking for help getting over your breakup—some sort of life preserver to get you through the next few bites off the wretched plate of despair that you're eating—well, you've come to the wrong place, compadre. This is where you're reminded that feelings are unwelcome intruders—a mosh pit of rude little enzymes dancing around in your gray matter.

If you've lost your girl, it's probably not your fault. Even highly imposing men have breakups. The important thing is how you comport yourself in the hours and days after your heart gets pulled through the jagged bone of that gaping fissure in your sternum. You didn't die, and quite frankly, there are bigger tragedies going on in the world, so you need to pull yourself together and show all of humanity that you are more than the sum of your dating experiences.

And this is how it's done:

DRINKING – You've all probably heard the cliché that "drinking never solves anything." That's what your mom told you, right? Well, it is sort of true, but you're not really looking for a cure here; you're trying to make an impression. As an imposing man, it's recommended for you to get sloppy drunk at least one time over a breakup. It's how real men grieve. After that, just drink four or five stiff ones per night to kill off the weaker brain cells. You should only drink hard liquor: scotch, bourbon, gin, rye, or tequila—never vodka, and beer is for gentler times. You might have another drinking preference, but you're going to have to put that on hold for now. How will it look if you're drowning your sorrows with vodka martinis or champagne cocktails? If you're a lightweight and prone to breaking open the waterworks after you have a few belts of booze, then you shouldn't drink at all, cupcake. Just empty half a bottle of whiskey into a mason jar and walk around pretending to guzzle the rest. When you see a passerby, make like you're taking a swig. It's not ideal, but if people don't see you drinking at all, they're going to worry about your feelings—and you can't have them thinking that you have any of those.

SOCIAL MEDIA – Here's a new thing that turns my stomach. When a man gets his heart broken, he is now overcome by the compulsion to announce it to the world via digital media. "I am so devastated by my breakup with @CoraJones that masturbation is not even an option right now." The fact of the matter is that you aren't going to win her back with a public estrogen dump, so shut the fuck up about your emotions. Assume she's watching you and knows what you're posting. After all, what better way for her to celebrate your agony with her friends than to read your Facebook wall or Twitter feed? Social media is a publicly accessible, permanent record of your current state of mind. It does not go away. Do you really want your social lessers to be able to punch in #myrtleloveache and be able to see 437 tweets that lay witness to your hysterics? Here are a few acceptable tweets that you can use if you can't think of anything on your own:

Bad week at work. Going to the gun range to blow off a little steam. @Greyson-Stone, want to come?

If that copier guy makes one more paper jam joke, I'm going to knock him the fuck out. #wrath

Does anyone know where I can buy a good #sharpeningstone for my edged weapons?

BRAWLING – On the exterior, you're the model of composure, but internally you're a seething, rage-fueled turbine engine. You want to kill someone, but if you do, you're just going to wind up on top of a wooden staircase at Tehachapi with a rope around your neck. Still, there's nothing wrong with a brawl or two to work out your angst. Actually, so long as greater numbers are involved, this may be the one time when it's even okey to lose a donnybrook. "Sure Cutter lost that fight. He was drunk and there were six of them. I think he might have dumped his girlfriend and she sent her goons after him."

COMMUNICATIONS – As a rule, once the breakup is done, you should not initiate any interactions with your ex. You probably need me to be more specific here: no face-to-face, telephonic, electronic, or written communications at all, frenchy. You may not leave a note somewhere hoping that she'll find it. You may not deliver a message through your friends or hers. Here are the situations where you can return her calls or correspondence:

She is claiming to be pregnant with your child. (Why get the lawyers involved?)

She has decided that she made a mistake in leaving you after she caught you with another woman and wants to beg for your forgiveness.

Her life is in danger. If this happens, you should only agree to help her reluctantly because you have a soft spot for dames who have been captured by highwaymen or pirates or whatever.

For a while, every time your phone rings, you're going to hope that it's her. It might actually even be her. If you don't answer, you win. I don't make these rules, but I do know that God gets nauseous when he sees a man breaking them.

REVENGE – There is no honor in physically harming a woman or damaging her property—ever. If you think you are likely to do either, please wait for my upcoming article *Seven Honor Suicides for the Imposing Man* where I discuss acceptable reasons for checking yourself out and cool lines to leave in your suicide note. In no way does this mean, however, that revenge is off the table. Among your acceptable recourses are:

Having sex with one of her best friends or a family member. If it's a family member, use the "One Generation Rule." No one is going to be impressed with you scoring with an adult woman's grandmother.

Emasculate her new boyfriend. You can accomplish this by either firing him from his job or fighting him over some bizarre insult. One caveat: this is a fight you have to win.

Challenge her new lover to a classic duel, but only over something that is completely unrelated to her. Do not disclose to your seconds that the reason you're fighting this duel is over losing a girl.

CLEANING HOUSE – Depending on how long the two of you dated, you probably have all kinds of pictures and tchotchkes scattered around your flat that you never wanted in the first place. Good riddance. Get a box or a garbage sack and unceremoniously toss anything that reminds you of her. If it has value, sell it or donate it to a charity. Along the same vein, your social media profiles are your public space and you should never allow someone who you are dating to intrude on them. If you have posted couple photos or allowed yourself to be tagged in them, you have to wait a little while before you take them off your feed. If you do it too quickly, she'll know she affected you, but if you wait too long, you look like some sort of goddamn sentimentalist or worse. Your best immediate solution is to post a lot of recent photos, effectively ramming the digital images of your broken romance down so far that no one will notice. For ideas of good post-breakup photos, friend request Vladimir Putin on Facebook. Whether he's posing with the world's largest Russian pikee, riding shirtless on a horse, or poisoning a political opponent, that man knows how to get over a breakup in style.

CHANCE ENCOUNTERS – No matter how hard you try to avoid her, there's always the possibility that she's going to sashay into some pub that you've never been to before or show up at a party that she didn't know was being held in your honor. Inevitably, she will look better than you've ever seen her look and be on the arm of some arrogant pansy with a fat wallet. Your first instinct might be to fill your hand with that snub-nose revolver you have tucked into your waistband or strapped to your ankle, but her new dandy is probably supporting a wife and kids. So, until you have all of the facts and a cold-blooded revenge plan, keep your weapon holstered.

Don't: Pretend like you didn't see her walk in. She knows you saw her, and acting like you didn't see her is embarrassing for everyone and undermines the fine work that you've done up until now.

Do: Be Gracious. "Listen, I was just headed to the bar. Can I buy the two of you a drink?" Say this whether or not it's a cash bar. If the idiot she's with challenges you on it, knock him the fuck out. Actually, you can punch him in the face at the slightest provocation. It's only bad form if you initiate the quarrel.

Listen, Nancy-boy, we don't want to hear about how bad you're hurting. We know: you're every stereotype in every mariachi song that's ever been written. Time to get back to whatever it is that you were doing before you met her.

Pull on your boots.

Stand on your feet.

Show the world no pain.

Be a man—an imposing man.

Traditional German Cuisine

There's a restaurant near my work that still has a smoking section, if you can believe such a thing still exists. I don't smoke, but I guess knowing that there are still a few places that spit in the face of "the establishment" and break the rules appeals to my rebellious streak. In addition to being one of the last bastions for tobacco enthusiasts in the city—maybe even the state—it is one of the only restaurants I know of where you can still get authentic German fare prepared and served by a staff of traditionally trained Black Forest gnomes.

Honestly, before I tried the Bavarian Table—that's the name of the restaurant—the most exotic food I'd eat would be maybe a burrito or pizza, but if you've never had a plate of Weißwurst with a big fat pretzel twisted by those little netherworldly hands, well, you just haven't really lived. They also have other things on the menu, but I tend to go for the simpler food. Every once in a while the manager will tell me that Willy, the Table's head chef, is feeling experimental and he'll push a taste of some new dish on me. Most of these items aren't even German—beet fried rice was particularly awful—and thankfully don't stay on the menu for too long. I'm not really a fan of beets, which gnomes seem to love to cook with for some reason, but as all dishes are made fresh, the cooks don't mind leaving them out if you tell the server when you order.

I think I failed to mention that the manager is also the owner and that his name is Yuri. His mother was a Russian and named him after his grandfather. Yuri is important because he's who I was talking to when I found out about the illegal smoking section. He told me that a while back he had discovered that the state tobacco inspector for this district ate in the restaurant with his wife, and Yuri and he had become friendly. One night, he was treating the couple to an after dinner nip of Bullenschluck when the official complained to his wife about never being able to enjoy an after dinner cigar. Yuri, who had always wanted to allow smoking in the dining room—he being a pipe man himself—suggested that the inspector and his wife just wait a few minutes for the other remaining table to leave, and he would lock the doors so they could all enjoy a nice smoke. He said it in a joking manner, but the inspector agreed. Apparently, some boozy deal was struck in that thick gray smoke, but I don't know any of the details of it.

The smoking thing doesn't usually affect me. The section is in a mostly enclosed room in the back, and I usually take a table for two by the front window, even when I don't have company. I always enjoy the street view: lots of pedestrian traffic and as far as the neighborhoods in this city go, it's one of the more scenic.

There was a point in time, I had just stopped going to the Table altogether. I had been through kind of a bad split with my girl, and my time was either spent in the furnished apartment I had leased after I was unceremoniously kicked out of her place, or out at bars where I would try to show the world how unaffected I was by the breakup. Looking back, my pain must have been pretty transparent, but we never know at the time, right? When I started to come out of my funk a little, I found it hard to find single women in my age demographic who weren't complete whack jobs, so I did what in retrospect was a relatively unwise thing: I started hitting dating websites. I think it was OK Cupid, Match.com, Plenty of Fish, and maybe one other. Not E-Harmony, though. All of those questions get tedious. I answered quite a few ads, but the one I want to talk about was this one:

Tired Of All The Games and BS! Looking for Prince Charming!

32-y-o woman, never been married w/ no kids. Non-smoker and would prefer the same. Hi! Are you tired of the same old same old? Lol. Well, so am I. I'm a fun, down to earth woman looking for someone that I have chemistry with. I'm easygoing and low maintenance. I like the beach, reading, yoga (NAMASTE! LOL!) and dining out at interesting restaurants. I'm not into games and I'm real. You be real too. Can you sweep me off my feet?

So, she seemed interesting enough, but it would be dishonest of me not to disclose that it was mostly her "profile pic"—street parlance for "photograph portrait"—that prompted me to send her that first message. After a few back and forths, we started to address the question of what she thought an "interesting restaurant" was, and as it turned out, she had only had German food once at a place called Spritzels in the mall, and it wasn't very good. I told her I knew Spritzels and there was really no comparison to the Bavarian Table, so we agreed to meet on a Thursday at around 7:30, which I thought was a good idea because if the evening went sour, I could get home at a decent hour and not waste a weekend night.

When we met that Thursday, it was almost immediately apparent that we weren't going to get along. To begin with, she was one of those women who likes to spell out her agenda right from the beginning: "I'm looking for a man to fall in love with, settle down, and have a family. My dream is to open a little boutique and I need someone who will support that vision— " She also made it very clear that she was "looking for Mr. Right, and not Mr. Right now." You get the point: it was just too soon. Also, she was a complete bigot about gnomes. In fairness, I didn't tell her in advance that the Table was a gnome restaurant and I seemed to remember that Spritzels wasn't. I just didn't think it was a big deal because I wasn't raised to think that way. And it wasn't even that she was one of those people who believed that all Black Forest gnomes were Nazi collaborators. (This, by the way, is not true. It was about fifty-fifty, and Yuri's family remained as decidedly anti-Nazi as anyone could during those dark times.) But, like I said, this had nothing to do with that. She kept freaking out whenever one of the servers would climb up on the table to pour a beer or offer a pretzel from his or her wee knotted fists. I mean, it's not like I could see anything that was so great about her meaty mitts. She also kept complaining about the smoking section, because as it turns out, she had recently quit smoking with Chantix™ and the little bit of smoke that was leaking out into the main dining room was giving her cravings for a cigarette.

I actually don't want to get into how bad the date was going because it's not all that relevant. Suffice it to say that we would not go out on a second date, but that could also be because of the circumstances that prevented us from finishing our dinner. At my request, Jason, the host, had seated us at a table by the window where we could enjoy the view. We were ordering our second drink from the bar when an old brown Buick Regal stopped in front of the restaurant and allowed a middle-aged woman in a summer dress to exit the rear passenger side door. As she walked further down the sidewalk, I noticed the Buick's windows rolling down, and two long black assault rifle barrels with fancy sights coming out and pointing at the restaurant's plate glass window.

No one has long to react in these situations, and I had a lot to accomplish in very little time. I knocked Yuri's nephew Barley, who was dancing a jig on a stool (poorly, I might add), to the ground by swiping his legs with my left hand. He went crashing to the floor hard, but he was otherwise safe. My date, who hadn't even noticed the car, looked annoyed at my attack on Barley and stopped telling me about her "ideal man list," which had to have been into maybe its hundredth item by this time. "And this is an absolute must have characteristic— What are you doing to that gnome?!" I responded by leaping across the table and tackling her backwards in her chair as the first rifle rounds penetrated the glass. I may not have liked her very much, but I draped my body over her like I was the soulmate for which she had been desperately searching the web. Our bodies were so close it felt like our hearts were beating in perfect but opposite time to one another.

In the madness of the crystalline blizzard that was raining down upon us, our eyes locked and I knew right then that I could fall in love with this beautiful gnome bigot if I just gave it a chance. I kissed her soft lips while I felt for the .38 special I carried in an ankle holster on my right leg. I'd kissed a lot of women before, and I've even been kissed by a few, but nothing ever felt like that desperate momentary buss with the bullets screaming through the air above our heads. When the action stopped, I rose up and fired a couple of rounds at the fleeing car, if only to mark it for law enforcement. When the hammer fell on an empty chamber, I looked down and knew that she was dead. One hateful missile had found its way to her lungs, and I had taken her last breath.

Now, you may have heard that some Black Forest gnomes have mysterious restorative powers and can even bring the dead back to life, but while Yuri's group could do amazing things with traditional German cuisine, they were useless with healing spells and incantations. My date would remain dead, but my entire meal was comped. I shelled out a fifty as a generous tip in gratitude for the establishment's largess, but I haven't been back.

MELISSA
NEWMAN-EVANS

photo by Marshall Goff

Melissa Newman-Evans was a member of the 2012 and 2014 Boston Poetry Slam at the Cantab Lounge slam teams. She co-coaches the Emerson College slam team with her partner Kevin Spak, she has headlined poetry shows around the northeast. Her work has been recently published in Muzzle, Radius, [PANK], decomP, and Freeze Ray. She likes her lipstick red.

Hidden Track

Becky, we decide, walks all from her hips.
Caitlin is all knees and elbows and neck,
and me--I am shoulders, like a linebacker,
like I am looking for someone to headbutt.

Probably because I am looking for someone to headbutt.
No one is happy when they are sixteen, and we are no exception.
It is midnight on a Friday, and we are not cool enough to even wonder
who can buy us liquor. We are singing songs from a musical that is our life,
which is not Rent, which makes us even bigger weirdos than than the theatre kids
on the next swing set over, but fuck them! At least we make up for our inability to carry
a tune
with unabashed volume. They will get cold and go home to their big empty houses by
one
And when they do, the world is ours.
This is the ceremony--

It is not brave to stay out late at night in the summer,
when sunlight reaches its sticky fingers late already and sunrise
comes for you so early. We stay out on the shortest day of the year,
in December where darkness spreads fat across our lives
and the cold breathes down our necks like death itself. We want to see all of it,
each other and ourselves.

By two, we are using the night to both see inside of ourselves
and to hide the fact that we have absconded
with two grocery store shopping carts
and are now riding them down the hill.

By three thirty in the morning, we are all geniuses.
We have invented a new genre of music and we are all singing the top forty;
the radio of our joy is loud as a jackhammer.
We are surprised by every minute that someone doesn't
wake up and call the cops on us for being too loud or too musical or
too bored or too happy in public without a permit.

By morning,
We have a mix cd we all share called Undertow.
It is compiled from songs that make all of us cry.
Every song is about something the singer can't have, or can't keep.
We listen to it and remember the little, comfortable unhappiness of morning.

But none of us will die from this loneliness.
God knows all of us will try in our own little half-committed ways,
but none of us will succeed. We will die eventually, but not from this.
We will not ask each other stupid questions when we show up at school
with some evidence hanging off our wrists;
We just carry the tune on louder when one of us falters.
Remind each other that morning is just a bearable weight.
Remind ourselves we are not singing for anyone else.

I walk from all points now
My shoulders,
my hips, my elbows and knees and throat.

This is the ceremony:

Think of the person who loved you before you deserved it.
Think of the people who got you through the worst.
You know who it is. Their name is a song you already know the words to.
Hold their name in your mouth. Sing.

Owning It (at 15)

For the 15 year old version of me, who cannot possibly be questioning her sexuality

In kindergarten, you chased down boys on the playground and tried to kiss them. You are positive this is proof you are straight, even though the kiss club you formed to chase those boys was always threatening to kiss each other.

I am not gonna tell you that *it gets better.* I am gonna tell you that it gets different. The world will move around you and you will move to a new school and a couple of years will change everything, whether you want it to or not. You can still only imagine being married to a man. Anything else is too hard and you're too lazy. Amanda is not going to be able to tell the difference between a compliment and a come-on when you tell her she's the sexiest girl you know. Stop pretending that you're only dancing with her because no boys will dance with you. Stop pretending that being called a dyke offends you because you have gay friends. Stop talking about your friends like they're the only queers you know.

Stop making that *lol i'm str8 tho* face. Straight girls don't wake up with your sticky fingers after a sleepover. Straight girls pull out the day bed. Straight girls, when asked, don't say yes to the threesome just so you get to watch his cock vanish inside of her with that face that says *I know what it looks like when she comes and she is faking it right now.*

Just because you didn't love her *right*, didn't love her with that dedicate a song on the radio pining, that stupid pointless public thing you keep throwing at boys doesn't mean you don't love her at all--you do.

You will have to remind yourself how queer you are daily. Don't say *not very.* Don't say *not enough.* Don't say *I haven't suffered to call myself that.* You will meet men someday who will fetishize your willingness to open your mouth and stuff both women and men inside, and you know you are not fucking women behind locked doors as a show for them. Being invisible, or a sideshow is a different kind of suffering. Your closet is made out of other people's assumptions. When they try to tell you what you are, tell them to get their preconceived notions out of your pants. Tell them that you are not here to entertain or to be silent. Your love does not answer to anyone.

Work Anthem

Work. It is the thing you are doing
because it is hard, and because
you need to. Maybe for the money.
Maybe because you want to run
from everything and the treadmill
is close enough. Maybe you have
to get stronger. Maybe you have
to get the words out. Maybe work
is just a thing that human beings
have to do, and you are, still, a
human being, and you are going
to prove it by working. Dancing is work.
Getting on stage is work. Writing poetry
is work. If you enjoy it, that does not mean
it is not work. It is work because
you have to do it, and it is hard,
and you are human, and you
are doing it anyway. Laughing
when crying would be easier:
work. Holding on to everyone
who loves you: work. Getting
out of bed in the morning: work.
It is not easy. It never will be. It is the
certainty that you have wiped down
this very counter three thousand
eight hundred and sixty-four times
and you will do it again tomorrow.
You will send the same form email
ten more times this week. You will run
the same route around your neighborhood
every morning. This routine is
the work: the endless routine.
It is not enough to do a job well
once and then rest on your laurels
for the rest of your life. Accolades are
boring. Your hands are ill suited to sitting idle.
Your feet want to move you forward.
Endurance is your birthright.
If you try to coast your way through life
like it is the waiting room for death,

the work will not wait with you.
A sense of purpose does not fly standby.
Your life and all the possibility in it will
outrun you if you let it, and nothing good
is going to rain down on you unless
you call down the thunderhead yourself.

There is a person inside of you
who wants you to stop working
this hard. He wants you to slow down,
hold up, wait a little longer, put it off
til tomorrow. He wants you to look at
the couch cushions. The bed. Your
beautiful pillows. That fucker has stolen
your face. Your time. Your life. Tell
him what happens to thieves in your
house. Show him how fast you can go.
Give him nothing but your dust cloud
and a sense of jealousy. Keep working.
Swing your fist. Tell distraction to go
take a nap. Tell compromise
to call back another day. Tell
defeat to fuck off. You are busy.
You are working. From now
until death comes to pry you
out of here with his hands. And Death
will have to catch up with you first.

JENNY OLSEN

My work is a meditation on the dark memories found in the face of familiar places-dreams and nightmares captured in black and white—a visual fairytale . . .

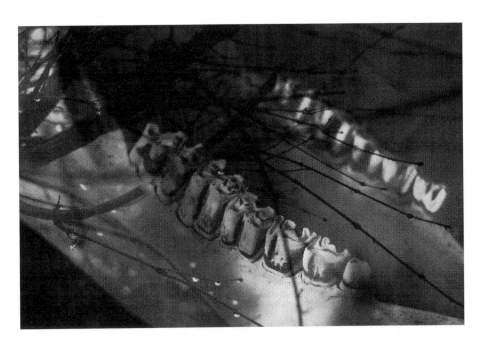

EMILY O' NEILL

is a writer, artist, and proud Jersey girl. Her debut collection, Pelican, was the inaugural winner of Yes Yes Books' Pamet River Prize. She teaches writing at the Boston Center for Adult Education and edits poetry for Wyvern Lit.

right to be hellish

after Nick Jonas

don't like passive people *honey does he*
love you really / how anger hides behind

homespun kindness *where he been*
if he's yours / everybody wants to taste

what they'd save themselves / ready
& jealous of sex in any form / turn my cheap

body more beautiful when you look / I'm excited
by obsessive attention / have you seen my man

present or aggressive / have you seen wishes
for an audience / will you look

away / taste disrespect *where he been* if
he's looking / if he saves nothing

is it your job to worry when he's taken
my knotted breath apart / *honey*

does he / hate the swarm
of invitations *if he's yours* turn

my cheap sweeter / you can't close the only
snare without my permission / let him run

wild on whoever says yes / no disrespect
in looking or getting what looks good

undressing attention until he's the only
one watching *where he been* besides hidden

in all your wishing / don't you want to save
a little sense to sip before he hears us

talking / *does he love* how they hover
when all faults are possible

music loud & I'm ready to hang up / *honey*
does he sip sense & anger in one sitting / call it reason
honey does he care only
for appearances / no he cares only

for being the only one you can see / can't face
what isn't his to taste / what makes me

mine / my right to breathe / to leave to start
what can't be finished / to post it all

my right to *honey does he* disappear

NJ Transit

This drunk summer I am girl
with the drugs. The barkeep at Hennessy's passes tight, tiny roaches
into my pockets like change for the payphone. Hands me an eighth
full of seeds when I say I'm not staying. The boys wait to trade
Quik Check subs for spliff smoke. We play the same drinking game
every humid night. Jug of barely-wine too heavy to hold
hovering at your lips. There's only one rule: set the bottle down /
lose a layer

shuck off damp t-shirt & jeans / fold your glasses into a sleeve / spill a pint of Jack on
the train / slip out of your socks / transfer in Seacaucus / diner gravy on your fingers /
handle of rum in your purse / peeping
frogs at the edge of the pool / chase /
catch / slip through my own fingers /
stink of chlorine / of salted August

They're fleeing of an already-bare house in North Bergen
but I've set up shop anyway, drowsy housefly
looping from one doorway to the next. Axel steals my underwear /
puts it on / jumps into the pool. One long night until it's not.
The season all boy-voiced. We shout & shout & groan
& argue & somehow I am never sick with sound, certain
drunk is the only door that opens onto relief.
The world, separated into brackets—VHS vs Britney
Spears / Kronenberg vs Carlo Rossi. Whatever
is oldest is winning. Whatever I've not seen in years /
                              I won't call mine

party with the Princeton Prep boys / this drunk summer / I am always last to leave /
I'll finish the wine reckless / square of chairs on the patio / naked with the stragglers /
mouth stained burgundy / don't stop until loss is impossible / I keep forgetting / an-
other sip / I am too young
to live this lonely / another sip / he left
me for a city with more cars than jobs /
he left me to swim in vinegar & ditch
weed like a slum rat / another sip /
lose a layer / another sip / & another

Everything to Everyone

I put myself in stupid places: Hampton Beach
Casino Ballroom, same shoes on for 18 hours. Nobody buckles

at the beach. Nobody worries swell will snap them like a wish-
bone. One half of me is napping, the other half yell-singing

"Father of Mine." My father didn't vanish before my anger crawled
with aphids, then flowered. Rage didn't die with him, only changed

shape. Who drew me a father without eyes? Was it his father
pulled over the night he was born, thrown into the drunk tank

slurring not from scotch but from thirst and didn't the cops
laugh in his crinkled face when he asked for a candy bar

and didn't Lee rescue him with the Hundred Grand in her purse
and deliver him to his only son? My grandmother wants me to believe

Owen only ever loved the track. Not her. Not his child. Dogs. Horses.
Paper tickets and the gates spring opening. Hating someone

when you're young is easy and endless. If I say I haven't
grieved this right, can you help me? Who hammered Dad's blindspot

into my teeth like a curb? When I'm on my feet all day, every day,
bruised in the hips, unwilling to touch anyone who hasn't seen me

shattered or shattering over this. Nobody gets behind the wheel
and asks to fall asleep. But I'm asking. Tell me when to stop.

SOPHIA PFAFF-SHALMIYEV

lives with her two children in NW Portland where she is freelancing, finishing writing her book, *] To Mother*, and applying for grants and fellowships now that her MFA thesis is done. Sophia writes about shame, bad luck, feminism, estranged mothers, bad heroes and hot ass.

If It Hasn't Been Yr Decade For A While

1. While pondering the subject of a woman's reputation, I have seen the aura before the blinding headaches more than ever lately. Squinting makes it feel better, but still, there's the popcorn machine sound behind the eyes. I want cotton balls drenched in ice-cold milk to plop into the dark veined sockets darting back and forth. Freeze out the barking dogs. Feet for eyes and eyes for feet to run through the steaming mud. As I get older, the offense is no longer as simple as calling a woman a derogatory word citing a sordid past. Those can be badges of courage; they can be yawns; a collective sigh. It's the pity, followed by erasure that is the next tight valve to burst in your future because you're a woman who is aging and you have been left.

2. It all began the day I read the first few lines of an article in the waiting room seven years ago. Back when I was still a therapist applying blame to the numb. Back when I believed Sartre and de Beauvoir were pure and the *New Yorker* article was the hook for this sinker.
John and Yoko.
Exene Cervenka and John Doe.
Kim Gordon and Thurston Moore.
Maggie Nelson and Nick Flynn.
The one who shot himself and the ugly one who lived and got the leftover hate, clothes torn off when she dove the stage.
They were supposed to make it, but the piles of togetherness-worship rubble make for taunting road signs.

3. I worry there's nowhere to return to and no way to un-know what happened to the couples of my youthful adoration. I will watch the flickering reel of John Lennon baking bread for his little son before finally going back to "real" work in the studio, to calm myself after reading of Yoko arranging for auxiliary female companions while he arranged for his opium deliveries.

4. Of course it was Sartre and the Beaver that I hoped were immune from the traps of a basic courtship before finding out what her freedom truly entailed. Their journals revealed a strange hate for the world they worked so hard to capture, transcribe, document and extract for meaning.

5. But let's examine the facts now so that parallels can be drawn. I will ask for no collusion or agreement on your part while you glance at this Rorschach test of relationship ink spills. This anxiety, these headaches, this perseveration of sliding the needle through the layers of fabric too thick to wear with any comfort will be a stitching of a garment meant only for the scratching closet.

6. The men of vision—Sartre and Flynn—one with a lazy eye and the other, with pierc-

ing blue eyes "of a derelict," using wartime as background rumination. Nick is swimming laps. Maggie is swimming laps. They both speak of breathing within Buddhist scripts. She writes of cruelty and he writes of torture, both gluing scraps to fragments as a writing practice.

7. Sartre and Beauvoir were a well-known literary couple who lived in Paris as teachers, mentors, scholars and inventors of a new kind of relationship, where true love was not marred by conventional walls of commitment, a nuclear family claustrophobia, a boring regulation-size kind of passion, suffocated by monogamy. They launched many divorces, journeys of self-discovery, and attempts at an enlightened beingness within the nothingness of ordinary life.

8. Nick Flynn woke up one day in love with two women at once. The words: woke up; the words: one day; the words: with two women at once—should have been mercifully extracted from the words: in love, but that's the story we get. That's the aura before the migraine. Clichés wrestled into philosophical explorations.

9. Sartre proposed a pact to the Beaver—their love would remain primary and finite, but they could seek pleasure outside the dyad, as long as they came back to each other and shared every detail of their conquests. They did it for laughs, as much as, for the now-anemic amorous tension.

10. I'm in the Andy Warhol camp of good times—my favorite part of a raucous and raunchy night is always the morning climb into my hungover friends' beds for a recap and recovery session. But as a woman I don't know which one came first—the guilt and shame, or the pleasure.

11. Ever since I found out I have taken to crossing out each Inez and Anna with a red pen and writing Lili and Maggie above them in Nick Flynn's book. Up until now I wasn't sure what purpose such a violent editing would serve, but it has been a corrective experience, removing a single thin layer of a harrowing silk heat emitting from my squinting eyes as I piece together their story.

12. Sartre would advise the Beaver that jealousy is the enemy of freedom. When his journals were released, the audience anticipating a gateway to a revolutionary attitude towards matrimony found out that he got the most satisfaction in the seduction, and little pleasure in the sex.

13. "Imagine, for example, someone who fucks like a whore," says Maggie about Nick. Indeed.

14. Just like the child who yearned and day dreamed after a divorce, the love may have become the triangle as the center.

15. While Maggie takes great care to never judge or be offensive towards the "other woman" in her otherwise candid work, Beauvoir writes the novel, *She Came to Stay*, in which she creates a character for herself to kill Sartre's favorite mistress, whom she sadistically renders as a tragic, incomplete vessel. The whole "second sex"—a foster family unable to adopt after locking their charges in the attic.

16. And so every week, Sartre made what he called his "medical rounds." Each woman he loved into submission had specified hours set aside to spend with him. His "mistresses" almost never knew about each other while living on the same street, and possibly bought their shampoo at the same pharmacies or tried to flag the same cab.

17. Nick describes Anna, but actually, Maggie, as always there, available for him to approach in the midnight hour, usually wearing a bathrobe. He tells her, *I'm not ready to be with anyone yet,* "not really." They feverishly discuss books, ideas, poetry, dreams shadows and light as writers who should be each other's true equals. When he disappears, the shadows need a place to stay and so he leaves them behind with Maggie while he goes on a first date with another woman, during which they "sort of discuss having children."

18. Sartre described the women he was attracted to as "drowning women," and believed their lives to be damaged or insecure, making it easier to get their full attention. Those who have read all of Maggie's works, as I have, are viscerally disturbed by the fact that he appears in some way or another in four of her books. They feel her attention could have been devoted to less sappy and predictable topics, and Nick Flynn's part in the narrative is too true and too vague at once to be called art.

19. In high school, I walked the hallways never saying hello to anyone because I needed glasses to see more than tunnels of bees smelling of gym socks. Once I finally got some, it turned out I had a reputation as a slut that began as a blindness. And so I took them off again and lost sight of the oncoming traffic on purpose, which didn't make it easier to escape, just hazier to take in as a snapshot of what it meant to be a marked creature. Being in the business of spade calling doesn't give you better cards.

20. If a guy, let's say, Nick Flynn, writes a book about you being left for a more stable woman, being a drunk, a crier at his breakfast table, patient and duped, or asking for rough sex he meets with patronizing refusal, or not being a blank enough wall—calm as a cultivator of cool wads of cotton balls to soothe his tired eyes—then what kind of blindness must afflict you upon looking. What kind of reputation must you dis-own then?

Waiting to be Emptied

Dear Marie,
Yr thighs are ruined, you want too much.

Dear Marie,
Pink.
Nineteen.
Nodding razors hello.
Glad folding pale slips.

Dear Marie,
I married the butcher to get to the bone.

Dear Marie,
Love letters to non-lovers is our inner dialogue melting the mint sting smell in the dark bar again.

Dear Marie,
Are you reading *Truth and Beauty* and wanting to make paper planes out of each and every ripped out page, then never fly them my way?

Dear Marie,
We were never lazy when we were still friends, because every couch cushion was on fire and clammy boy hands swatted away ashes faster than the burns could appear on our thighs.

Dear Marie,
If temperate climates are the ones to incubate the future of footsteps then why did this happen to my cold cold cold spring?

Dear Marie,
I left you because the wrapping cracked on the record meant we start talking about the nature of circles again.

Dear Marie,
Diary entries.
Lecture hall.
Only two seats.

Dear Marie,
And now on to wrestle dust to dust to make water for my letters to soak.

Dear Marie,
Inland bravery before shipwrecks.

Dear Marie,
Neither one could offer a brother for blood, laying down a towel as we do.

Dear Marie,
Knots the sheets in the nightly escape.
Curtsy to every prey before lay.

Dear Marie,
I may have stared at your throat then and saw a necklace of hellos getting smaller.

Dear Marie,
Stop painting pictures of us with the clouds scarlet white.

Dear Marie,
Don't you sleep in the cold if you want to wake up.

Dear Marie,
I may have told you that there's no such thing as sharp magnets in nature but there always awaits an edge to each stone.

Dear Marie,
Larvae to egg, larvae to egg, larvae to egg.
Crawl back my sweet baby.

Dear Marie,
My milk in a bag. And yours, powdered to suck.

Dear Marie,
Birch tree forest grown so dense and so tight the torn papers are slapping each other.

Dear Marie,
I believed the red ribbons you tied in your hair and passed down the food chain.

Dear Marie,
Lucite heels on wet floors at the glass box place. Irony stole the heat in the pile up of nervous rejections.

Dear Marie,
Parched, never thirsty.

Dear Marie,
Or, I remind you that champagne, it is made out of tap water.

Dear Marie,
This hangover tastes like our desert, so dry and so proud.

Dear Marie,
That will always be us climbing cherry trees in nightgowns opened wide, and a lunchbox with Old Golds for inhaling the blight on the branch.

KATHERINE PIVODA

is preoccupied with language and secretly wishes she was Helene Cixous. She enjoys bad jokes and cheap wine and spending too much money on books. She is also fascinated by post-modern ennui, goat cheese, and pictures of baby bears. She recently received her MA in literature from the University of Colorado Denver because street cred, yo. Feel free to send her an unsolicited dick pic.

STILL LIFE WITH BABY'S ARM: a critical analysis of the modern art of the dick pic

When Robert (32, Thornton, CO) sent me a picture of his genitals, I admit that I clicked on the thumbnail without much more than mild curiosity. Having received more than my fair share of these manly self-portraits over the years, I must admit I've developed a keen and discerning eye when it comes to the male anatomy. Honestly, I think no girl is better versed in the art of dick-pic deciphering than one who has attempted online dating several times. No matter how earnest or sweet you make your profile, you will wind up with at least a couple of penises in your inbox. Men seem to love nothing more than grabbing their hard-on, snapping a selfie, and sending it to me. What was remarkable about Robert's dick-pic was that he had included a TV remote for scale. There his hard-on was, veiny and straining against the skin that contained it, a hairy hand barely visible in the bottom of the frame, some kind of watch cut off by the camera angle. And right next to Robert's throbbing monster was his universal TV remote, obviously designed to handle flat-screen, plasma television, cable, blue-ray, high-definition, etc. What struck me about this strange (and for me, heretofore un-encountered) juxtaposition was the situation Robert must have found himself in: no access to a ruler, glancing wildly around his living room for something to make his dick look big. I pictured him, this man who used his first and last name in his email address but neglected to send me a picture of his face. He was probably watching a ballgame on his clearly elaborate media setup. I imagined his hairy arms brushing against his dick once, twice, and finally he decides to masturbate. Was he masturbating to my personal ad? I don't know. But I do know that once he reached his full, turgid glory, Robert slapped his dick down next to his TV remote and took a picture to send to me.

Most dick pics are fairly standard. Once in awhile, you get a glimpse of abs or t-shirt (tangentially, I feel there must be some statistic that correlates Hollister brand shirts with likelihood to send an internet stranger a dick-pic, because Hollister is disproportionately represented), but usually it is just a sad, strange, lonely dick, weirdly curving against the blurry background of some dude's messy bedroom. Placed side by side, lined up in rows that make quick comparisons easy, one is struck by how similar most dick-pics are. Of course, there are variances between size and tilt, girth, whether or not he is circumcised, and especially treatment of pubic hair, but most men take their dick-pics from the same angle: laying down, dick in foreground, camera angled up to capture the majesty of their cocks.

A few men violate this formula: standing up, they will take the picture looking down at their dick. This is most disconcerting because it works the same way as a POV porno, and the only real difference is that suddenly I'm sharing a perspective with someone who has a raging boner and feels the need to take a picture of it. Oftentimes, these gents don't even remove their clothing. Jon (27, Boston, MA) left his socks on in what was possibly the least sexy dick-pic I've ever seen. His cock was lean and curved, clearly winter-pale, nestled in a burst of wiry brown pubic hair. But it was Jon's also winter-pale legs, ending in bright white tube socks and covered with disconcertingly dark hair, that dominated the picture. He was not wearing any pants. It would be one thing if, like Colin (24, Ann Arbor, MI), Jon had simply unbuttoned his pants and pulled his penis out. Colin's unzipped fly and unbuckled belt were clearly visible in his snapshot, and his dick looked as if it had sprung, fully-formed, from his Fruit-of-the-Loom boxer briefs. He had (wisely, in my opinion) left his testicles inside his underwear so I didn't have to see them. Jon, however, went to the trouble of completely removing his pants and shorts, but he left his pristine socks on. It was a strange kind of disconcerting: if Jon and I had any sort of sexual encounter, he would clearly be the type to leave his socks on. This, for me, is unacceptable, and also, for a 27-year-old man, kind of a bummer.

The picture that ultimately made me the saddest, though, was Ryan's (22, San Diego, CA). Ryan emailed me two photos: in the first, a doe-eyed boy stares longingly at the camera. His dark hair is longer than it should be, and his goatee hugs his chin like it's scared of something. Ryan is wearing a dark gray t-shirt and has exquisite cheekbones. I remember opening it and thinking, "What a good-looking, soulful kid this Ryan seems to be!" The next photograph, however, was Ryan's penis. It was thin and long and wholly unremarkable but for the fact that it clearly belonged to the sad and serious 22-year-old in the first picture. Now, I haven't met anyone who can't enjoy a good game of Guess-the-Dick, in which participants drink too much white wine and speculate about the size and shape of genitals belonging to strangers at the bar, but getting photo confirmation that Ryan's dick was as sad and skinny as he was filled me with a strange melancholy. In his email, Ryan included various details about his life and hobbies, including the fact that he plays acoustic guitar and is trying to decide whether he should go back to school or continue his exciting life as a line cook at a Mexican Restaurant. He skateboards everywhere. Unlike most men, Ryan presented himself as a complete person, face shot and life details included. And I couldn't help but mentally add to his self-evaluation that he was also the kind of guy who sent strangers (me!) pictures of his dick.

Why did this make me so sad? Perhaps I was struck by the un-ironic eagerness that Ryan's email portrayed. Grammatical capabilities aside, Ryan seemed to be legitimately looking to someone to connect with. And somehow he thought that sending a picture of his penis would make it happen. Ryan didn't want to tongue my pussy until I was dripping wet, or flip me over and slip his huge dick inside me, or lick the soft petals of my womanhood so I could explode in his mouth, all of which were romantic activities various other men with penis pictures proposed. Instead, Ryan wanted to take me out for tacos and play me the guitar. He wanted a girlfriend, someone he could listen to shitty punk-rock with and then go out for ice cream. Ryan was a hand-holder. And it was with genuine unease that I let his email stagnate in my inbox, along with pictures of less sensitive men holding their trouser-snakes up to cans of Red Bull in attempts to prove their unending virility, while I contemplated Ryan-the-boy versus Ryan's penis, and how strange the two seemed in relation to one another.

Admittedly, this thought-process threw me into a bit of agonized existentialism. How could Ryan, a somewhat-articulate real person, feel like his dick could be a game-

132

changer? Why did he think a girl like me would be more likely to go out to dinner if I already had a picture of his cock? In what universe could I recognize and relate to poor Ryan's as he attached both photos to his email and hit 'send'? In what universe could I ever start a relationship with someone when I knew they send strangers pictures of their intimate bits? What kind of a person actually uses this as a dating strategy?!

While I thought about emailing Ryan back, I never did. The types of questions I wanted to ask would probably go unanswered unless we shared a taco dinner, and frankly, it was too much commitment for me. Instead, I consoled (and amused) myself with Steve's (47, Denver, CO) sad and drooping testicles, which he managed to capture in a mirror. I looked at Christopher's (34, Boca Raton, FL) epically tanned and seemingly strutting erection. I even clicked on Brian's (31, Seattle, WA) sad, stubby, circumcised self-portrait. In short, I consoled myself with a world of stranger penis, made stranger by the fact that each one of them probably had a backstory like Ryan's. They, too, cultivated hobbies like tennis, or they loved to read, or they were proud of their ability to make pesto pizza for a girl that they liked. But, thankfully, instead of sending me a brief breakdown of their passions, most of these men opted for a succinct photo attachment in which they highlighted what, in their opinion, was their best feature.

Ultimately, like most women with dick-pic saturated inboxes, I eventually realized that any man who wanted to show me his cock first and foremost was just not my type. Perhaps in the course of a year or two, snugly cohabitating and being in love, I could see myself requesting a sexy portrait of my man's parts. But until then, stranger dick remains a strange and kind of gross way to get to know someone over the internet. Intimate in its connotations but sadly lacking in any kind of context, a man's penis is, I think, the least comfortable chunk of himself he can document. Feminism routinely discusses the ramifications of body parts: when we look only at a woman's breasts or legs or belly, we forget to acknowledge her existence as a complete person. Men, conversely and in a gross generalization, seem to crave this kind of dissection: they want their cocks to represent them. Most men who emailed me pictures of their penises felt that their photos would be proof enough of their worthiness. As a woman, I have spent a generous chunk of my adult life rebelling against my body, trying my damndest to rise above the reductive ramifications of a big cup size and a pretty face. What astonishes me was the fact that men legitimately use their genitals as stand-ins, assuming that the swaggering and swaying dick rising proudly in the foreground of their cell phone shot is a good enough reason for me to email them back. This, I recognize now, is where phrases like "cocksure" come from: men can—and routinely do—view their cocks as miniature representations of them, absurd though these pornographic selfies are.

This is representational art at its most distilled, natural form. This is Van Gogh's veiny and striving starry night. This is Michelangelo attempting to touch god. This is Ryan's soul and his shitty iPhone camera is his canvas. This is all about connection and impression. Kandinsky would have waved his cock in a circle and snapped it at the perfect apex. I am just an unpaid critic or patron at the museum on opening night craning my neck and wondering about the motivation of the artist, before I eventually shrug and give up and go get more wine.

I Would Tell Betty Freidan to Suck It But I Am Pretty Sure I Got There First: A Modern Ethical Slut vs. The Feminine Mystique

"The problem lay buried, unspoken, for many years in the minds of American women. It was a strange stirring, a sense of dissatisfaction, a yearning that women suffered..."

This summer, I found myself confronted with an unusually long period of completely intimidating free time. Once summer classes ended, the only activity I had scheduled for July and August was sitting in the empty coffee shop I worked at, gazing longingly into the distance, and possibly reading books. As someone who is perpetually paralyzed by the thought of boredom, those swaths of summertime read like a gaping maw threatening to swallow my entire existence, tempting me with time-wastes and binge-drinking. I knew that if I wasn't proactive, my only recollections of this summer would be wearing all the sweat-pants and watching Oprah.

I wish I could blame my attempt to read *The Feminine Mystique* on the suggestion of an educated and well-meaning friend, but the impulse came from one too many feminist theory classes and my lifelong ambition to be the most interesting person in the room. So, settling into my patio one evening in late June, a glass of Pinot Grigio in hand, I cracked open Betty Friedan, entirely prepared to have impressed upon me the full weight of white women's issues in mid-century America.

Over the next few days, I couldn't help but notice how long the book was. My edition contained 417 small print pages articulating the female struggle. The chapters had titles like: "The Happy Housewife Heroine" and "The Sex-Seekers". The entire book was filled with scenarios I couldn't help but associate with my late grandmother, whose opinion on feminism I never asked, but who ran my extended family like the martini-drunk matriarch she was. I was also stuck thinking about my mother, who I happen to consider one of my best friends, and who also was inadvertently affected by Betty Friedan's astute and frighteningly political assessment of female being. If nothing else, *The Feminine Mystique* proved an intimidating book only because it threatened to bring me into terrifyingly intimate contact with women who I had long swore were my absolute opposites.

I should preface this study by admitting I'm kind of a slut. By admitting that there have been men upset by the fact that I call myself a slut. By admitting that there are certainly men I regret sleeping with. I should also preface this study by hoping (with words and feelings) that my father never reads this, and that, if he does, he forgives me. There are things that I, as a sexually liberated woman, have never admitted. These things include the intonations my grandmother always had: "Why buy the cow, if he gets the milk for free?" "I wonder who she's kissing now...." They were followed by my mother's inevitably more subtle approach: "Who are you dating?" "Did he buy you dinner?" "What does he do?"

After The Divorce (capitalized because nothing else means much when you're a kid and your parents stop loving and living with each other), my sexuality became something I could barter with, and not just with boys. Climbing into the cab of my father's pick-up truck one night, I remember him yelling at me about losing my virginity. *How could HIS daughter, do THAT*, he insisted. I slid my body out of his truck, feeling less like a girl than a lizard. Back then, I was pretty convinced that if anything got cut off, I would be able to grow it back again, that everything was fixable, that regeneration and redefinition were a normal lesson in growing up. I'm only recognizing now I may have been wrong.

I tend to think I managed to become a decent daughter. My father lives in Ohio now; my mother stays in the same city I grew up in. We drink wine together far too often. We talk about my sex life and I pretend her insides don't wince every time I mention I've slept with someone new. For me, it isn't complicated. I like having sex. I like having orgasms. I like having orgasms with people I have sex with. For her, it still seems to be a conundrum: on the one hand, she is feminist-proud of how able I've been to own my own vagina. On the other, I'm fairly sure she's disgusted by my debauchery.

As Friedan points out in one of her long ass chapters, Freudian sex-politics are one of the things that led to the whole gendered struggle in mid-century America. As I like to casually admit with a shrug, these things can all be reduced to Daddy Issues. Or Mommy Issues. Or maybe issues that inevitably arise from an ever-changing cultural landscape. I don't mean to be reductive, but earlier tonight I was accused of being too terrified of vulnerability to ever be a decent writer. While I'd like not to think that vulnerability plays any sort of mitigable role in terms of my skill, I'd simultaneously rather be honest than a hater. And so here it is, thrust out on a table like so many autopsied bodies that once held meaning: this shit is balls.

What I mean is that: I started an OKCupid account to ostensibly discuss Friedan in terms of what we've made the modern day woman. I was pithy and clever in my summations of self; I went on a whole week's worth of dates (at least.) I slept with more men than I should have, had I remembered my grandmother's advice. And at the end of it all, I was still left with "the feeling that had no name". But it was a pervasive ennui that had already invaded every sort of person I knew, man and woman. This sticky feeling that can't be summed up in words or experiences, but rather viscerally, in chest cavities and deep inside our stomachs. We all share it, like Friedan's desperate white housewives, except for now we have thick-rimmed glasses and all the irony, and actually being vulnerable is something honest and hard and scoffable, because it's so much easier to do things indifferently.

The chilling sense I get from my generation, and the generations surrounding it, is that we are fucking miserable. Miserably miserable. The kind of miserable that finds no resolution in articulation. "Jesus, what a bummer!" we all seem to mean, riding our bikes or driving our used cars or living in still-carpeted apartments. This is not to say we would all improve greatly from an influx of cash (though we like to think we would.) We would be so much better if the whole world got on our page. We would be so much better if God didn't really exist, if organic milk was a right rather than a privilege, if dudes didn't feel the constant need to justify their low-carb diet to me. Rather than this, though, we are too good at settling, too good at lowered expectations. We are too good at big-screened TVs and microbrews, too good at claiming meaning outright, like we ever had something to do with it. Too good at never having to buy the cow, too good at giving the milk away for free.

This summer, confronted by boredom, I read most of Betty Friedan. I hated myself for a while. I hated my parents for a little bit longer. The more confronted I felt, however, the more constricted: sex is maybe an answer, but it can only be one. My orgasms do not wave the liberation flag like once they might have. Rather, in a post-modern world, they have taken on more ambiguous meaning. My straining hips beneath sheets carry nothing but the man who tries them on for fun. I feel constantly like I have managed to taint just the idea of meaning with my breath while simultaneously advocating for it like some suckah who believes in God. I am alive, after all, beneath all this. And I wish so organically I had a better conclusion.

My original hope was to read Betty Friedan freely, and costlessly. I am, after all, an educated white woman. I hoped the book would educate me. I hoped the book would provide enough stark juxtaposition for me to begin to navigate my own existence in terms of sexuality and the modern age. I hoped that the book wouldn't prove folly, gender-roles worthless, that maybe truth one time existed and we just decided to ignore it. I hoped that by pressing something old up against something new I could extract meaning, like oil from olives, but all I was left with was a vague sense of oppressive and requisite honesty.

There have always been touches that approximate closeness. There are snarky anecdotes I will forever tell my friends. There are stories and funny names and things that have happened that land me at my girlfriends' table. High school tableau: please approve. There is also a strange sense of desperation, of justification, of admonishment. No one cares whether or not I fuck him; if they do, they wonder out loud how good it was for me. Or they wonder in secret how good it was for me. How big was it, Katy? What did he do to you, Katy? Do you really like him, Katy?

They never know what I always think: In my grandmother's voice: No one ever wants the milk, Katy. In my mother's voice: What does he do, Katy?

Always truck cab slippery, like too-rubbed vinyl beneath calloused hands. Asphalt beneath teenage shoes, high-tops with holes in the bottom. Loss registering like a cut-off tail: you can grow it back, but will it ever look quite the same.

BARUCH PORRAS-HERNANDEZ

Baruch Porras Hernandez is a Queer Mexican in love with Gummy Bears, Whiskey, and Allergy Medicine. He was born in Mexico, raised by the hippies and hot tubs of Berkeley and now organizes literary events in the San Francisco Bay Area. He is a Lambda Literary Fellow in Poetry, his favorite Gem is Garnet.

As A Gay Man It Is Good To Have Goals

Goal: Get the Macklemore haircut that everybody in fucking San Francisco fucking has
    Lose 150 pounds
    Keep beard
    Get tats
    Then only hang out quietly and mysteriously
    with other gay tatted-skinny-hipsterbeards
    stare off into space like baristas trying too hard to pretend not to care.

Goal: Lose 150 pounds. Get a spiky gay haircut with frosted tips
    Wear nothing but shorts and polo shirts. Call all my male friends, bro
    Ignore all women. Only talk to men if we are talking about how to make money
    Buy a giant house after displacing poor people. Never use it
    Kick brown children off of public soccer fields
    Slut shame men who are in open relationships
    Make fun of the word polyamory, have anonymous sex at the gym
    Go to Burning man
    My favorite movies will be Oceans 11 and Wolf of Wall Street
    Talk about how much I like HBOs Looking, people should really give it another
chance
    Post pictures of myself at pool parties surrounded by gay men that look like me
    staring off into space like a poodle that has eaten too much dog food.

Goal: Lose all the weight, all of it. Stop using deodorant
    Stop using toilet paper cause it kills trees
    Let 20 year olds live in my house but only if I can fuck them
    Have orgies, dye my hair purple and green
    rename myself Acorn Thistle
    eat so much Kale that I can't move
    stare off into space like a baby that is farting itself to sleep.

Goal: Lose 100 pounds. Buy more hair products
    Tan on the beaches of Brazil. Magically get my accent back
    Open a chain of Mexican restaurants. Buy my parents a house, each
    Fund all of the quinceañeras
    Party till I drop in Vegas for no reason
    Put posters of Scarface in Living room bedroom and kitchen
    Follow Ricky Martin on twitter.
    Become friends with Ricky Martin
    Seduce, make love to, break his heart, then leave Ricky Martin
    Ricky Martin writes a new bunch of love songs to me,

they teach the world to love after heartbreak
the only way a powerful gay Latino man can
As I listen to them in my house in the Hamptons,
I eat a bowl of cereal, staring off into space
like Maria Felix when she was bored out of her mind,
covered in jewels.

Christopher Columbus And I Play Gay Chicken

Me: *You're going down CC.*
CC: *Come on, I'm Christopher Columbus!*
I'm pretty sure I'm better than you at all things gay.

We're on the roof of the cathedral where he's buried in Seville.

CC: *I played gay chicken with Cortez on this roof just the other day.*
Me: *Who won?*
CC: *Wouldn't you like to know.*

The closer we get to each other, the more we try to throw each other off
by saying, sexy things!

CC: *Boy, you make me wanna discover that ass!*
even though it has been back there, behind you, the whole time!

We have an intergenerational multicultural Bromance.

Me: *Ooh You make me wanna turn all your people into salves,*
and rock their world!

One of our favorite games is to take a shot
every time we see a statue of him.

CC: *Boy! You make me wanna force you to search for gold,*
then when you don't find it, rape your wife in front of you
then kill your children.

We're pretty much drunk all the time.

Me: *Damn you're so fucking hot, you make me want to launch*
one of the largest waves of genocide known to history.

We get very close, our noses are touching.

Me: *Do you feel it? The statue I have for you, …in my pants?*

We kiss, then jump back. In silence,
we hold hands and start to fly back to the hotel.
Things are awkward, but I'm not worried.

It was just a harmless game of drunk gay chicken,
with Christopher Columbus' ghost, who is my BFF,
and if I've learned anything from him,
it's that if you give people enough time,

everyone forgets.

Dating Tips For Lonely Gay Men

When my friend is out on a date,
I text message him things he should say
to make the date go better.

-Tell him he is like apples, crisp and sweet, you like apple juice,
Say you wanna sit him on the head of small boy
and stab an arrow through him.
If that doesn't work, just whisper the word, Anal. -

-Tell him he is the nuts on your coconut donut,
you want to part the walls of his jelly roll
peel him like a fruit roll up
    Anal.-

-Tell him you will never leave him even
if he gets evicted and loses his job and has
to get food stamps, and can't go to brunch anymore
cause the connection is all you need, love is free
and so is
    Anal. -

-Tell him you're so into him you'd be willing
to listen to Katy Perry all day, especially during
    Anal.-

-Tell him your skills include gently caressing
his balls in your mouth with your tongue
while simultaneously cutting you both
a piece of pie out of the fridge cause you're a
multitasking kinda man,
    Anal.-

-Tell him he is an island, you are rain drops on the palm trees
he is barefoot, you are sand between his toes,
he is a tropical blowjob, you swallow, and or
    Anal.-

-Tell him you believe in gay rights
  his right to make you a sandwich.
    Anal. -

-Tell him our gay ancestors didn't die for our freedom
   so you to have to wait till the second date,
   for some Anal-

-Tell him when he gets old, you'll most likely leave him
for a 24 year old toxic twink who has a career in the tech industry
and already owns a house, but you two can still be friends right?
          Anal. -

-Tell him he has nice eyes. –

DOUGLAS POWELL (ROSCOE BURNEMS)

2014 National Poetry Slam Champion, poet, teaching artist, and father. For info, books, albums, and/or booking go to www.roscoeb.webs.com

Conquering Depression

Stare at yourself in the mirror, naked. Point out everything you love about yourself, then everything you hate, physical or or not. Realize the mind and the body are similar in the sense that they are both made of clay and you have a potter's hands.

Hide everything sharp: knives, scissors, razors, mistakes, and regrets. Your veins cannot purge it out.

Cry. Salt water and sand builds castles; Pack yourself tight. Depression comes in waves. Construct a strong foundation in knowing this too shall pass.

Breathe.

Lie to yourself. Lie until all the lies sound honest Lie to your lies. Make them believe they can be real boys some day. Tell them every time their nose grows they are 1 inch closer to cutting the strings. Repeat "I am not depressed. Depression is death and I am alive. I am alive. I live."

Love.
Be honest.
Be honest to your loves.
Love honestly.
Let honest loves love you.

Look at the sky when you walk. You won't be able to on first attempt. Your self esteem has been a pinched nerve, but patience heals.

Do not waste your time wishing for better days. Wishing is for stars and children. Wishing won't get you anywhere. Wishing will keep you there. Wishing has no follow through. Wishing is a verb, but wishing is not action.

Write. Read the suicide note you've scribbled down aloud in your room. Read it in a horrible Jamaican accent, then read it like you've inhaled a mouth full of puns. Read it ridiculous, until you can't take your blue funk seriously anymore.

Write. until your hands can only grip pencils, pens, and loved ones.
Write: you are more than Vicodin and Hennessey, more than nameless orgasms, more than the notches carved into wrists and thighs. more than your last words to a loaded chamber.

Write.
Breathe.

Stare.
Breathe.
Write.
Love.
Live.

And... And... And...

This poem ends when *you* say it does.

The list ends when *you* say.

> Walter Scott 50

When the names are more call to action

> Bernard Moore 62

When the names are clots of blood in your throat

and wounds in your flesh

> Lavall Hall 25, Jonathan Ryan Paul 42

When they become battle scar and war cry

> Jamie Croom 31

When the names are no longer just tear drops in a pool.

When they stop becoming trendy

When you are finally reminded it is genocide

> Terry Garnett Jr. 37, Monique Jenee Deckard 43

When you are reminded it is maafa

When you see the holocaust as a holocaust

and not headline.

> Tony Terrell Robinson Jr. 19, Tyrone Ryerson Lawrence 45, Naeschylus Vinzant 37

When we stop closing the discussions on race in America. Only then will the list close.

When police no longer cower behind judges, cackle behind badges, holster their bias and prejudice, and mistake it for their taser.

Only then will there be no faceless names for the news to vulture

> Andrew Anthony Williams 48, Dewayne Deshawn Ward Jr. 29, Ledarius Williams 23

When we stop making celebrities of carcasses killed carelessly and left to rot in a decaying judicial system.

When the ages stop sounding like jersey numbers.

> Yvette Henderson 38, Edward Donnell Bright, Sr. 56, Thomas Allen Jr. 34

It is as if America has run out of brick, out of chain link, and are creating walls with the bodies it has stacked...

> Fednel Rhinvil 25, Shaquille C. Barrow 20

The list is too long to keep using figurative language...

because the names themselves are metaphors

for the lack of respect brown bodies receive...

Kendre Omari Alston 16, Brandon Jones 18, Darrell "Hubbard" Gatewood 47, Cornelius J. Parker 28, Ian Sherrod 40, Jermonte Fletcher 33, Darin Hutchins 26, Glenn C. Lewis 37, Calvon A. Reid 39, Tiano Meton 25, Demaris Turner 29, Isaac Holmes 19, A'Donte Washington 16, Terry Price 41, Stanley Lamar Grant 38, Askari Roberts 35, Dewayne Carr 42, Terrance Moxley 29, Theodore Johnson 64, Cedrick Lamont Bishop 30, Anthony Hill 27, Terence D. Walker 21, Janisha Fonville 20, Phillip Watkins 23, Anthony Bess 49, Desmond Luster, Sr. 45, James Howard Allen 74, Natasha McKenna 37, Herbert Hill 26, Markell Atkins 36, Kavonda Earl Payton 39, Rodney Walker 23, Donte Sowell 27, Mario A. Jordan 34, Artago Damon Howard 36, Andre Larone Murphy Sr. 42, Marcus Ryan Golden 24, Brian Pickett 26, Hashim Hanif Ibn Abdul-Rasheed 41, Ronald Sneed 31, Leslie Sapp III 47, Matthew Ajibade 22, Charley Leundeu Keunang, "Africa" 43 and... and... and...

Stop me whenever you're ready.

Physics Lesson for Officer Darren Wilson, The Cop Who Shot Unarmed Mike Brown Six Times in Ferguson, Missouri

In physics, thermal radiation by objects or bodies
can be measured as blackbody radiation.
The term "blackbody radiation" describes an object that
radiates internally at the same temperature as its environment.

Kevlar and steel badge make you more frigid;
you… don't radiate at the same temperature as the bodies
you are sworn to protect.
Your temperature, a degree below inhumane,
too low to understand brilliant black bodies in Ferguson
or to see that Mike was not a black hole in search to consume six more.

Blackbody radiation emits light, though it appears black,
as most of the energy cannot be perceived by the human eye.
You, were too "human" to see his
  black body,
  human.
All naive adrenaline.
His imperfections outshining his future emanating inside.
In nature, no blackbody is perfect.
No
  body is perfect.

Insulated enclosures contain blackbody radiation
only emitting a light when a hole is made in its wall.
Big Mike was a large body.
Large
  black
    body.
6'4", 300 lbs of energy they never trained you
to harness,
would need way more than one hole in him
to see all the shine within.

Why is it our black bodies never seem to stay enclosed
around
  police?
The bright-blue burning in our bosom

blackened by bright blue flashing lights.
We have been forced to not reflect,
just absorb bullets and beatings.
For centuries, we have been trying to gleam bright enough for laws
to know we are more than dark unknown boiling to be incandescent.

We marched with the logic
the more black bodies, the more glow.
Boycotted as if taking away our light
would show you how dark this world is without us.
Our riots weren't violent; they were ultra-violet.
But here we are still just embers after gun smoke.

Some scientists say blackbody radiation doesn't exist;
But Michael was another star plucked from the darkness,
and Ferguson is more luminous than ever,
blazing bright with piercing protests and bodies so sick of swallowing abuse
that they've become volcanic.

Proof,
that action will always have reaction;
light will always have refraction.
And beware of what you beam at black bodies,
you may not be prepared for what beams back!

JEREMY RADIN

Jeremy Radin is a poet/actor living in Los Angeles. His first book, "Slow Dance with Sasquatch," is available from Write Bloody Publishing. You may have seen him on "It's Always Sunny in Philadelphia" or "CSI" or "Zoey 101" or in a restaurant aggressively eating pancakes by himself.

Champion

after Wislawa Szymborska

I champion silver.

I champion ferocious dunks.

I champion pumpkin everything.

I champion divinity unadvertised.

I champion terror over numb.

I champion all of the donuts
over some of the donuts.

I champion &.

I champion Portland & its grieving weather.

I champion my sister slutting it up in a slutty dress
over her modestly emptying her lust into the toilet.

I champion Brent's Deli to Jerry's Deli & if you don't, I champion a swift education.

I hope to champion survival
over pretending to be alive.

I champion Yiddish.

I champion *more work*.

I champion Shakespeare disrespected & vibrating
over Shakespeare awed about & still.

I champion the everything of doing nothing.

I champion a God that takes you up into arms
over a God that asks you to take up arms.

I champion the ocean at night & a blanket over my shoulders & hot black coffee

& not having to try to feel holy.

I champion my anger at my mother over my anger at my father.

I champion a warm bed in a cold room.

I champion listening over politics.

I champion sex
over whatever I'm doing right now.

I champion haunted windmills.

I champion the image of a beast swinging through the trees
over the image of my father staring straight ahead in a chair.

I champion open.

I champion Johanna, those freckles just left of the center of her neck.

I champion saying *when it rains it whores* when my sister tells me
she's courting three men over saying nothing on the floor of her closet
as she tries to court whatever gives her power to continue.

I champion continuing.

I champion continuing over everything else.

After Botching the Big End-of-the-Night Kiss You Drive Home Over Mulholland Drive, Listening to Leonard Cohen & Weeping with Relief

Blessed Idiot. Anointed Know-Nothing.
    What was it you said? I feel like I'm going
to kiss you now. & Valentine's Day. & stars
        sawing their violas. Even in Los Angeles
            the hushed beeping of frogs. O, tender
        beeping. The night unreasonably warm,
like the atmosphere around a pot of tea. I feel
        like I'm going to kiss you now. Sanctified
            Moron. Hallelujah Shit-For-Brains. & then
        the weeping. Leonard singing like a jaguar
chomping a fossil. Had to be people I hated,
        he sings, had to be no one at all. Ghosts
            licking honey from your heart, a light
        lifting like dust off the city. I feel like I'm going
to kiss you now. Glory, the screw-up. Numb-
        skull, glory. Unsnarling her cardigan from
            your eyes, one cerulean thread at a time.
        Lost in the night-hair, winding through its braided
sheets, & braided into your own body, tighter,
        tighter, until you don't know the difference
            between your body & the curses you've
braided into it. I feel like I'm going to kiss
you now. Divine doofus. Sainted schmuck.
        Consecrated fuckfuckfuck. Failure buzzing
            around your fat fingers. Failure entombing
        your obsolete sex. Failure like a shaggy
angel chewing your longing apart. O child
        of failure. Child of gracelessness. Child
            choking on the altar's absence. You said
        There's no way this was going to happen
with any semblance of elegance, & turned
        toward the sidewalk, leaving the hallway,
            leaving her bewildered in front of her door,
        your hearts, a pair of flickering lamps, a-frenzy
to settle on a condition. I feel like I'm going
        to kiss you now. & she laughed & backed
            away, said Why did you say anything, & how

could you tell her? That in that moment
a messenger lodged in your throat, sang
        this temple of clumsiness into you. O gift.
            O votive. O benediction. Ordaining you
        this hallowed klutz. Your tongue, a burst
of fevered moths hurtling toward any light,
        biting through the ink-slick strings lashing
            your limbs to the fingers of loneliness, yes,
        carrying you up, up, away from the dark
of the bordering day, from your yearning that she
        were some other she, & she, certainly, yearning
            the same, & up, & up, into that sprawled
        & glimmering gloom, tears like lamplight
gushing from your eyes, a bright old man
        exalting your ineptitude, the Name lacing
            the space around you, a perfect thanks
        blazing from your lips.

The Bull Speaks

after Maurice Sendak & Leonard Cohen

Leonard Cohen is my favorite.
What a perfect voice. I think he is right
about the Name. Leonard says

Without the Name I bear false witness to the glory. Then I am this false witness. Then let me continue.
Please

                                    give me
                                    a moment.

I have to be The Bull. I must be the only one
                                    who can bear it.

For ten years, I ate
only weapons. Axes. Rifles. Atom bombs.

     Longing, Max. That is all I am
                              ever talking about.

Imagine aching to gather everything into arms that look like this.

Leonard says so many glittering things.

We are ugly but we have the music.

& how his ugliness sees so deeply into mine.
Perhaps mine
can see this deeply into yours.

Perhaps we are the expression
of an ugliness shaped by paradise.
Perhaps we are the Proof.

The final hallelujah
of a dying star.

*so why do you lean me here / Lord of my life / lean me at this table / in the middle of the night /
wondering / how to be beautiful*

Bewilderment, Max. That is all you are

required to demand of yourself.
The Name, only spoken
in the failing
at the Name.
We are only a brief bewilderment of space.

Too fleeting to see how time is wasted   pushing happiness
down the throat of a species
                            not finished grieving
what it's done
in the name
of happiness.

            Ten whole years, I ate
        only weapons
                            & still...

O Max, I did
                        my best.
I have failed
                    with such devotion.

O Friend, do not be afraid
            of me
but with me.

APRIL RANGER

photo by Sam Ranger

April Ranger is a Brooklyn-based poet and playwright.

What The Poet/Waitress Works For

Money, I know, is an ugly word
to put in poems, can't we keep commerce
out of anything? The answer is no,
not even love. In love, you paid
for a new strong wheel when my bike
was robbed and I was broke. In love,
I cried the first time we shopped for groceries
together, all those fresh organic herbs,
nine-dollar handmade beeswax candles. In love
you listened every time I told you
I cannot afford. In love, you paid
for our escape to Montreal, city
of turquoise shutters and bright cafes.
In love, I asked *how did you not know*
green peppers are the cheapest?
In love, you told me I wouldn't always be a waitress
and I thought you were ashamed of my life.
In love, I bought expensive miso
because you liked it on your sandwiches.
In love we cooked at home instead.
In love we swam at night, for free.
In love you moved from Cambridge
to the outskirts of JP. In love we loved with our bodies,
all, over, loud, and with our own damn heat.
In love we turned and roiled in our sheets,
in love we gave and gave and
gave and gave and gave.

The Poet/Waitress In Love with an Art Critic's Son

"They say - and I am very willing to believe it - that it is difficult to know oneself - but it isn't easy to paint oneself either."

Vincent Van Gogh, letter to his brother

We were about to make a home together,
so I threw out my favorite painting.
He would cry if he knew.
His art was authentic and I was ashamed.

I threw out my favorite painting,
a print from a thriftstore.
His art was authentic and I was ashamed
of loving something so simple.

When I saw it at the thriftstore,
my heart remembered itself.
Loving something so simple
made me feel rich in solitude.

My heart remembered itself
whenever he spoke in my ear.
We were rich in our solitude.
I hated my old, singular life.

Whenever he spoke in my ear,
we were making a home together.
I hated my old, singular life.
I would have cried if I knew.

What A Minute Is Worth

"Juan got me in trouble for clocking him out early.
I mean it was like, one minute. Seriously?"

-- Manager of my restaurant

So many kisses. Anywhere from one
incredibly long, sea-deep mouth dive
to maybe seventy-five short ones, where lips
skim the body the way a good rock
touches the surface of a bay.

I've had a one-minute back-rub
change the course of a whole night.
I mean, my whole life. Last year
I saw a man leap into subway tracks

to pull a woman who fell,
just before a train avalanched
through the station. But time
is not only for heroes and lovers.

A minute is good
for one stream of piss
and washing the hands.
The fully-fleshed daydream.
Clouds that change shape
seven times and disappear.
Watching the letter burn.

A belly laugh that lasts
long as a full minute
is the reason we work,
the reason we keep on.
This has never been
about money.

JESS RIZKALLAH

is a Lebanese-American writer, illustrator, and coffee slinger living in Boston. She graduated from Lesley University, edits Maps For Teeth magazine, and publishes zines and chapbooks at pizza pi press. Talk to her about whales.

i left the light on two minutes past dusk and now mortality is trick or treating in my neighborhood

it knows now: this house is not the shadow it hides behind
it is a vessel bursting in amber, biology suspended

& my family members like fingers
animating the house from the inside,
they're finding the holes in the fabric,
breaking the fourth wall to raise the blinds

they marvel out the windows
at all the Trick or Treat *Look at the Trick or Treat!*
the American intensity of holiday
of all the extra steps taken to erode the sweet tooth
to make for a rot that splits the bone down the middle
holes so deep   an inhale catches death
in the molar   a stubborn seed not yet swallowed

& in the kitchen, my grandmother's hand with a knife
over the liver of a goat alive this morning but now between
the blade and chopping block atop the kitchen counter
this thing that once determined
a creature's buck and ball
being cubed onto a clean plate.

it looks like canned cranberry sauce the Americans eat,
just cut a different way.

& the goat's heart on the floral dish next to the anise liquor:
this thing that once determined the hum of something's blood
now a bald metaphor waiting to be fried in all its butchered glory,
its valves hollow, the color of my lips   & my lips the color
of every woman scorned   her blush drawing blood
from the scorners, i store it in the creases my teeth
can never get to when i bite at the pigment
around my mouth

i am always one lopsided pentagram away from an offering
& a punchline. this is always a punchline:
how i am always one kissed napkin away

from a crime scene   i am always prepared
for a crime scene, but never by nature's hand
knocking at my door   & its polite pause
before picking the lock

i'm hiding razors in the moments it's come to pry open

like this one here: my uncle pouring shots
while my mother decorates a different
raw animal with purple onions and sprigs of mint.
this is common practice. something i can never explain
to my vegan friends. a sentimental sacrifice
& the alcohol a jovial killer of anything hiding
in the meat.
we will swallow the poison
and feel warm

& the next room: my grandfather a transistor. a light flickering,
telling ghost stories of rotary phones & three dollars a minute
letters between beirut & goddamned columbus' soil,
how it wasn't even his   & how sentiment took months
to travel and that was all you had
months and that's all he has

this is his birthday: this feast. this meal, this offering of another year
lived medium well and everyone's here but still
there is someone at the door.

loud enough for the persistent shadow to hear,
my grandfather says
"I'm going to eat this fucking liver
& I'm going to digest this raw meat
I'm going to drink this aged anise
& what a fucking sham I'll never see
my mountains swallow the moon again
what a trick that I'll die on this land/what a joke
what a farce/what a sick twisted end of a blade
into my navel but also   what a full table.
what a full heart. how lucky i am. that the hollow thing
on the table is not yet my heart upon a dinner plate.
my organs chased by liquor
how happy i am that you're all here. let's have a toast.
keskoun, kilkoun. allah khalili yekoun, may God
lengthen your lives into unbroken windchimes, & hey

164

Happy Halloween while we're at it! and hey
your friends are never going to believe you about
that goat heart   dig in

if teta never had to leave lebanon i wonder if she would make preserves

the middle east wasn't called the middle east before the west started calling it that.

i learned this three years into college, twenty-one years into the first generation,
and so many poems deep about how this region is a cat   back and forth
under the DNA propping up my blood.

i could stop calling it the middle east   i could call it Mediterranean
i could call it kitchen counter in the sunlight
tiny lizards napping in the window sill / parsley straining in the sink
i could call it abdel halim-hafiz tuning my mother's heart from the radio
teta's apples becoming vinegar under the sink
jido's mountains swallowing the moon every morning

but why would i dignify the history books by letting them think all this remnant is Art.
the collection of small miracles i call home is just the pinking skin around a scab
where once, the earth was a mouth laughing like lutes and molasses.

why would we let the west think this jagged wound a birthmark, like it was here all along

they don't teach it like this: a toddler dipping into the fingerpaint innards of the cat
rubbing it on the fridge, smiling up at you stupidly, like this is art.
they teach it like: stupid cat for being a trusting predator.
for sleeping belly exposed.
not stupid toddler. never stupid
toddler.

poetry workshops tell me to be less Poetry about my rage
poetry workshops also tell me to be less poetry in my poetry
to never let the poem know I'm talking about it, *never let it know*
where you are, what it is, don't talk
about writing. never talk about writing, this is a game
to play while your people burn. today in the sun   tomorrow too
but the next day they'll be leather on the tectonic hot plate
under the west's tongue / under the hiccup holding a pen,
drawing new lines where the earth was already wrinkled.

they call the zig-zagged eastern border between Jordan and Saudi Arabia
"Winston's Hiccup." Churchill once boasted of his "liquid lunch,"
of "creating Jordan with a stroke of the pen one Sunday afternoon in Cairo"
are you joking

they tell me to be less cosmic megafauna about it, less phantoms wielding scalpels,
less filling   but more cavity over the already boring down
to the DNA held in my mouth when i speak   they tell me to just fucking say it

sometimes there is nothing left to say.   sometimes
there are just mountains struggling to breathe / just abdel halim hafiz singing revolution
from the kitchen counter   his heart stuck in the static's throat
and the overwhelming twitch of the fingers into a fist, of the squeeze around the pen

sometimes there is only the bubble on the job applications
where you fill in the circle next to   "white/middle-eastern"
because you're working hard   you're a good American today.
you get to be white today. you're white when you're behaving
you're a terrorist when you're angry
   you're a liar when they wound you
you're stupid when you're sleeping,   you're a predator
            when you're backed into a corner.

you are the earth's oldest apples
you are DNA becoming vinegar under the kitchen sink
venom under the tongue   something you didn't put there
something you'll always be spitting out.

Sin el Fil, Lebanon

1.

i asked her to tell me something about the elephants
she told me she used to live in one of their teeth
burrowed into beirut like a forgotten cavity
it's where her mother had cancer and her dog ran into traffic
the year before she met my grandfather

i asked her about the curve of the tusk at the base
of their home, she said they stood there
huddled, three days, bricks for pillows, sirens
replacing the birds   and fingers coming through
the ground for the ankles not yet twisted by the rubble

the next day, they made for america
and thirty years later, the ivory is still in the basement
cocooned by a silk curtain.

2.

i asked him about the beginning of the war
he told me about the people walking over
broken glass   how everyone in the city seemed
some sort of Jesus, with shards of what would
one day floss the Mediterranean
getting caught in their heels

i asked him about his first and only pet
a german shephard.   *rin tin tin,*
a name like three sharpened teeth in a row
before a bite into the west's ankle   a mark made
above the boot coming down   , a heel too soft
to know the carve of its own flesh

i guess we have always worn our pain proudly

3.

he told me about mortality's breath
the matted fur between his children's arms
the organs like disintegrating pottery
when the refugees fed the dog shrapnel

he whimpered at the door til he was found,
abdomen giving way to scarlet fingers
red sea parted by his tongue and the final heave
before his body became a prophecy
for every cedar and every person
every cedar lives inside of

4.

they scoff at the american attachment to animals
at how their new neighbors take the predator into their home
how they clean its shit and hold it when the night
remembers itself at their door.

as boston thaws over the morning dog walkers, i count all the ways
i have come to understand the distance my family keeps

                        when enough homes collapse into mines,
                        anything close enough to lick your
                        wounds will sound like a canary.

5.

she asks me why i keep asking about the elephants,
why i love them even though i can never hold them
i tell her about the toenails and teeth, the tusks
and their bones everywhere, like these stories

and how they're something to know from afar,
and something to watch die from afar
leaving behind their bodies as shelter.

i ask her how many years it would take to visit each grave
the past filled to bring me here. she tells me i am full of these graves,
that each day i am here is a flower left at a different stone.

OLIVER MICHAEL ROBERTSON

is an artist, illustrator, musician and graphic designer with a degree in graphic design from Portland State University. I am passionate about art and illustration and am always looking for new ways to express myself through different media including etchings, engravings, woodcuts, pencil, pen and ink, painting, colored pencil and the piano.

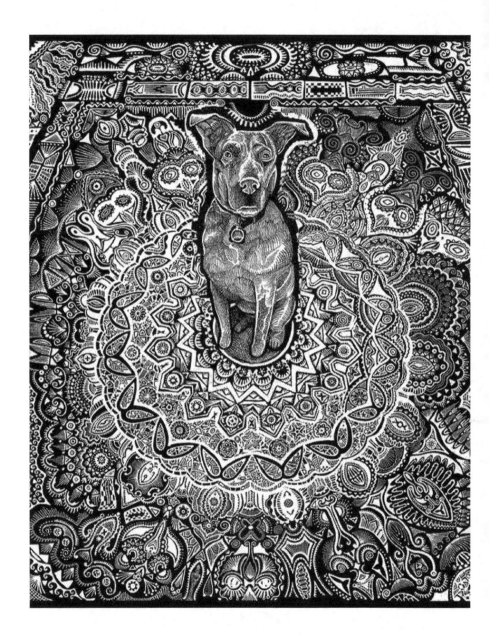

MELANIE ROBINSON

graduated with a Bachelor of Arts in English with a concentration in professional writing and a Minor in Anthropology from the University of Texas at San Antonio. She is a poet, musician, journalist and marketing extraordinaire, in order of importance. She holds the title of Marketing Manager at ARTS San Antonio and is a freelance journalist with the *Rivard Report* and the *San Antonio Current*. To say she dabbles in the arts would be a gross misrepresentation of the neurotic beauty she finds in self expression.

The Melanie Manual of Don't Fuck with me: The Handbook of Handling Too Closely

If I am crash test jungle gym,
If you are smiling theme park carousel,

how do I starry eyes and where is start?
What if I can't?

I tried a few times. I know how to "out of my league." I know when to leave – could teach you a thing or two about not worth it.

If I am tile factory stampede,
If you are brick laying balancing act,

how does one stay?

Why do they look like drifting or
Southern Comfort and black jack?

What is content without angry? When is apology, how do I sorry?

If I am shotgun shell,
If you are streetlight 2 am walk home,

what is forgive me?
I am 23 and don't know how to do this properly.

Can someone teach me human and dream and good enough and keep?

Why are we are so disposable?

Drunk Texts to Ichabod Crane

Wicked people tell the best stories.
Meet me in Hell.
Let's make it 10:30. Just jump on 35 and ride it till you hit Persephone. Take a left
somewhere between life and decay. A gnarled trunk of splinters will be waiting for you
there.
Thousands of skulls
tethered to its limbs
whispering breeze through hollowed sockets of purgatory
There are days when I stand like a two by four
just to watch the
…swinging…

We're more alike than you think.
More make believe and dying, too drunk to take the next breath, who needs air
when we have all this
burning?

Can I tell you a secret?

I want you to tip toe the Salem back into the tombstones of my tailbone.
You should come over.
Sleep with a demon, feel the gallop in my spine, taste the bits of Dahmer.
Do me a favor –
inhale this rigor mortis pretty as an inkblot eulogy. Hold it in your ribcage while I inci-
sor this one-night stand to gut wrench the banshee between you and me.

This is abandoned house me. Me in chains.

I think I'm dying.

I am dreaming of touch lately - and strangers kissing.

I made slaughter to you,
I hoped you would stay.

Jibber Jabber

Wordswordswordswordswordswordswordswordswordswordswordsword-
swordswordswordswordswordswordswordswordswordswordsorwordswordsword-
swordswordswordswordswordswordswordsperhapswordswordswordsword-
swordswordswordswordswordswordswordswordswordswordswordsword-
swordswordswordswordswordswordswordswordswordswordswordsword-
swordswordswordswordswordswordswordswordswordswordswordsword-
swordswordswordswordswordswordswordswordswordswordswordsword-
swordswordswordswordswordswordswordswordswordswordswordsword-
swordswordswordswordswordswordswordswordswordswordswordsword-
swordswordswordswordswordswordswordswordswordswordswordsword-
swordswordswordswordswordswordswordswordswordswordswordsword-
swordswordswordswordswordswordswordswordyou'llwordswordswordswords
wordswordswordswordswordswordswordswordswordswordswordsword-
swordswordswordswordswordswordswordswordswordswordswordsword-
swordswordswordswordswordswordswordsfindwordswordswordswordsword-
swordswordswordswordswordswordswordswordswordswordswordsword-
swordswordswordswordswordswordswordswordswordswordswordsword-
swordswordswordswordswordswordswordswordswordswordswordsword-
swordswordswordswordswordswordswordswordswordswordswordsword-
swordswordswordswordswordswordswordsitwordswordswordswordsword-
swordswordswordswordswordswasn'twordswordswordswordswordswordswordswo
rdswordswordswordswordswordswordswordswordswordswordswordsword-
swordswordswordstillwordswordswordswordswordswordswordswordsword-
swordswordswordswordswordswordswordswordswordsyouwordswordsword-
swordswordswordswordswordswordswordswordswordswordswordsword-
swordswordswordswordswordswordswordswordswordswordswordsword-
swordswordswordswordswordswordswordswordswordswordswordsword-
swordswordswordswordswordswordswordswordswordswordswordsword-
swordswordswordswordswordswordswordswordswordswordsholdword-
swordswordswordswordswordswordswordswordswordswordswordsword-
swordswordswordswordswordswordswordswordswordswordswordsword-
swordswordswordswordswordswordswordsitwordswordswordswordswordsword-
swordswordswordswordswordswordswordswordswordswordswordsword-
swordswordswordswordswordswordswordswordswordswordswordsword-
swordswordswithwordswordswordswordswordswordswordswordsword-
swordswordswordswordswordswordswordswordswordswordswordsword-
swordswordswordswordswordswordswordswordswordswordswordsword-
swordswordswordswordswordswordswordswordswordswordswordsword-
swordswordswordsyourwordswordswordswordswordswordswordsword-
swordswordswordswordswordswordswordswordswordswordswordsword-
swordswordswordswordswordswordswordswordswordswordswordsword-
swordswordswordswordswordswordswordswordswordswordswordswordsmouth-

wordswordswordswordswordswordswordswordswordswordswordswordsword-
swordswordswordswordswordswordswordswordswordswordswordsword-
swordswordswordswordswordswordswordswordswordswordswordsword-
swordswordswordswordswordswordswordswordswordswordswordsword-
swordswordswordsandwordswordswordswordswordswordswordswordsword-
swordswordswordswordswordswordswordswordswordswordswordsword-
swordswordsswallow.

MEGGIE ROYER

is a triplet from Iowa who is currently attending Macalester College to major in Psychology, with possible minors in Creative Writing and Women's Gender and Sexuality Studies, and in her non-studying free time enjoys eating macaroni and cheese and surfing etsy for cool new finds. She has been writing poetry for about three years now, and won two national medals for poetry and a writing portfolio in the 2013 Scholastic Art & Writing Awards. In addition, she is the founder and editor-in-chief of *Persephone's Daughters*, a literary journal dedicated to empowering abused women.

@ **The Poet I Become When I Drink**

Look, we both know everyone in your life who knows better
is glad your 21st birthday doesn't fall on a Friday.
But the truth is, you'll still party anyway
soak your angel cake in alcohol then light the candles
& the whole thing will go up in flames.
And you'll say fuck it
and gorge on all the ashes
as long as they're enough to get you drunk.
What was it you did at 20? A whole year with only a few shards
to remember. That's what addiction does.
Mourning the eight inches of hair you cut off
& the man-shaped mold someone left on the only moon
you could see from your front window.
Can't even remember his name now. Chances are,
it was just a one-night stand.
Chances are, the whole time you two were kissing
you were blacked out.

On Having a Boyfriend with OCD

He was always turning the oven on and off,
opening and closing the door,
counting as he went: thirty-seven, thirty-eight, thirty-nine, forty.
Eventually I had to tell him that if he kept opening the door,
we'd have a whole bunch of house intruders
before the night was through.
He responded by trying to kiss me once,
then ended up kissing me twenty-three times, then once more
for an even twenty-four. Then he had to redo two of them
because "our mouths hadn't been quite aligned."
Needless to say, this involved some swooning on my part.
Some nights I'd wake up with the moon soaking the bed sheets,
listening to the sound of him repeating the word "fuck"
over and over: he'd stubbed his toe on the bathroom doorway
but couldn't stop swearing once he'd started.
I fell back asleep after staring at my pillow
until the floral pattern burned into my eyelids,
dreamt the two of us went to an opera but instead of beautiful,
tremulous voices rising high into the air,
two sopranos were singing "fuck" to the tune of La Traviata.
He apologizes the next day, says the new medication
made him feel like shit all the time so he took himself off it;
I respond that it probably made him feel that way
because it was working.
Two days later the ambulance comes and takes him away;
he'd accidentally cut one of his wrists with the steak knife
chopping carrots for stew
but couldn't have just one cut wrist;
he had to have two.

Past Lives

As a child you believed the phrase mother tongue so deeply
that you once opened her mouth and peered inside
to see if language was a tangible thing nestled between her molars.
In the treehouse before the boy next door came up
you lay over the knotted wood like a starfish,
waiting for him to open up your ribs
and find the dark red hidden inside.
The day he moved, you looked into your own mouth in the mirror
and tugged out the third molar from the left,
strung it up over your bedpost
to ward off his ghost.

CARRIE RUDZINSKI

photo by Rich Beaubien

is an introvert, anti-socks activist, feminist, candle maker, juice queen, filmmaker, published author, world traveler, and internationally renowned performance poet. She has represented Boston, Denver, and Los Angeles over the course of 11 national poetry competitions and published 4 collections of work since she began performing 10 years ago.

October

The weekend after I moved to London
my boyfriend broke up with me. I'd left
a month earlier to backpack around
Europe and finally worked up the nerve
to tell my parents that Jon and I were dating
and would be living in the same apartment
next year all in the same breath. On the last
stretch of I-90 between the Des Plaines Oasis
and O'hare; *Bye! See you in five months.*
Maybe I told them because he had been so
distant since I last saw him. When he asked
why I didn't want to touch him in the dark.
Couldn't see the way I crawled into myself.
Couldn't find the voice the others had swallowed.
Couldn't tell him I hardly knew him, that love
so often felt like a child watching a puppy
through the glass. That I abandoned my body
before I ever found it. That I didn't feel anything
when he touched me. I was still a small boat adrift
in the sunshine of the weeks we started falling
asleep in each other's beds, waking up
at dawn to watch the sunrise. Couldn't
tell him my sex wasn't something I had
discovered yet. Couldn't explain I needed
to move slowly through the dark with him.
So I left my voice in the bathroom.
Ran the water like a shadow and cried.
Couldn't say what was wrong with me.
Didn't know I'd believe there was something wrong
with me every day after that night.
When he broke up with me, walking
through the new Autumn night, he did it sloppy.
A wet band aid abandoned at the pool.
Something he'd decided months before. Let me
uncork myself on a cold stoop in Camden Town.
Slurred voices barreling past us, a shattered
phone booth, the street lamp that wouldn't
let me stop shaking, my voice a ripped
photograph. I wonder if someone living
in those apartments peered down
and saw us, finally naked.

A crumpled girl unable to bandage
her howling. And a boy,
waiting to leave.

Survival

When you get called "Sir"
for the dozenth time
in two weeks/
you cry/ briefly/
while dragging your suitcase
through the underbelly of Los Angeles's
Union Station/ and wonder if only
you had worn a tank top today/
maybe you wouldn't be crying.
But she looked you in the face/
this time/ took in all 14 hours of travel
your body endured just to get here/
to buy this bus ticket. You/
with two bobby pins in your hair/
you with your faded blue hoodie on/
you with your impossibly tight skinny jeans/
she was a foot away from your face
when she asked, "One way, Sir?"

And it's as if the blood
was never enough. As if
the men who have chased you
down the street, hollered, or laughed,
or begged, or used their bodies
as a weapon against you
just disappeared. As if you
didn't understand the paradox
of needing to be attractive
but not too attractive.
As if you didn't already feel
unattractive most of the time.
As if the day your male boss
said you should have worn more
clothes to work meant nothing.
As if you weren't immediately aware
you were being sexualized
and being told it was your fault.
As if you were born Temptress.
Witch. Object. Apple.
Let your mouth
be a swarm of protests/

a night of cicadas:
it will still be your fault.

As if at your college internship
you didn't have to get everyone's lunch
while the male intern got to actually learn something.
As if you've never ran home
like your name was thank God
it hasn't happened to me
yet.
As if you didn't flinch every single time
a man or a group of men or a car full of men
or a city block of men or a nation of men
called out to you/ because they knew
you would flinch.
Because of everything that has come before.
Because you are a womyn who is alive.
Because not all men, but enough men.
Because the good ones/ aren't telling the bad ones
to stop.

As if you are nothing more than your gender.
As if everyone has a gender.
As if calling someone "Ma'am" or "Sir" is necessary.
It's not.
Every sentence you say with those words in it
will make sense without those words.
What can I get for you?
Would you like some sugar?
Are you buying a one-way ticket?

The worst part about being called "Sir"
is when you correct someone.
And you say, "I am a Womyn."
And they laugh/ before apologizing.
As your body isn't something you live inside of.
As if your request to be called what you want
to be called isn't important. As if you
haven't just been surviving/
enough/ already.

The Hallucination

Love is a boy with addictions
to everything but me. Love
sounds just like a dial tone.
Love knows he is my first
want. He is a field waiting
to be grazed. Love taught me
to forgive like a wing ripped
from its socket. Love taught me
patience carries a knife. To walk
like a bruise blooming. To devour
each lie and ask for another.

I found a toothbrush
that is not mine
in Love's bathroom.
Love is a salt block of excuses.
A scab I chewed through.
Love makes me walk home.
Love is forgiven.

Love taught me how to drown quiet.
So I may taste how to flood.
So his hands are the last thing
I kiss. Love is forgiven.

Love is a severed finger
forgotten in my pocket.
I wait. And wait.
He never calls.
Love is forgiven.

Love has too much desire
and not enough hands.
He wrapped his mouth in a telephone wire.
Promised not to kill himself
this time. Love says I am his
but he is not mine. My love
is malignant. His mouth is all
of the reasons I flinch
when other men touch me.
Love taught me to wait.

I am old now.
Love is forgiven.

Love did not mean it.
Love tells me all of his secrets.
Love refuses to kiss me in public.
Love is only sober when he is with me.
Love is a breeze in everyone's skirt.
A handprint on the inside of my thigh.
Love tells me he loved me too much.
Love never apologized.
Love is broken.
Love told me his mouth
is the last train home.
Love knows I am not
his Love. Love told me
not to love him.

But how do you claw
your way out of the river
when you are a stone?

SAM SAX

is a 2015 NEA Fellow and a Poetry Fellow at The Michener Center for Writers where he serves as the Editor-in-chief of Bat City Review. He's the author of the chapbooks, *A Guide to Undressing Your Monsters* (Button Poetry, 2014) + *sad boy / detective*(Winner of the Black Lawrence's 2014 Black River Chapbook Prize). His poems are forthcoming in Boston Review, Indiana Review, Ninth Letter, Poetry, Salt Hill + other journals.

Teeth

how elegant, the disarticulated human skull
where steel makes one fused bone many.

the mandible is a planter's box outside my cold room in ohio:
the converted nursing home where old folks from poland
and romania are all now trapped in the lights
or trapped in the white paint.

*

antique sciences of the mouth
can teach the history of science
more than anything about the mouth.
for centuries lancets and leaches
were used on infant gums
to assist teething, animal bone rattles
drowned in mercury powder,
a white gloved hand doing damage
in a child's bright mouth.

*

my teeth are mine. felt them rise up under my tongue.
wisdom came last. replaced each tiny forbearer.

forgot they grew where their parents died. so i am not
surprised they ache and rot now, they scream when flooded
with something sweet they do not deserve.

this is what happens when you forget your history,
the journey that brought you to the mouth, the labor
in the enamel, the tongue with no name,

when all you are is white.

I Dare You.

try & watch a horror film
from the point of view
of the monster. imagine,
every man shrieks at the
sight of you, children throw
stones & laugh at your
blood, a mob forms on your
doorstep   with pitchforks
& forceps just for fun or for
fear. this   is your wretched
life. you didn't know your
name   until they named
you. didn't know your teeth
were fangs until they tried to
pry them from your pliant
skull, didn't know your
hunger was so unclean. so
you learned to grow in the
dark as darkness grew in
you. your mirror   a
massacre of light, your
appearance   a film reel
warping in flame. it's not
until you love a boy & make
him like you that you're able
to curse the civilization that
assembled your fiction, to
gaze upon your own
grotesque elegance & laugh,
to love the rough hewn
battle of your haggard
breath. you child of the axe
blade   wheezing in
your breast, you story men
tell to explain away   the
darkness & give it depth.
you apotheosis of the oldest
protest hymn. what is the
ocean besides a puddle
without you in it? what is
the grim forest besides a

factory   of trees praying
to be shorn into paper?
what is   your mouth
but a home, but   a
haunted motel, but a siren of
terrible righteous noise. now
the men who tormented
you, tremble at your sound.
& when you're finally ready
to spread wide your wild red
wings, it ends. some idiot
girl pierces your faggot
carapace   with her car,
or sword,   or word in a
dead language for fun or for
fear   &   audiences   in
darkened theatres release a
collective sigh as you perish,
as credits roll back like eyes
& you're reminded this is a
movie, that you die onscreen
every night. try & get to that
last scene without laughing
or weeping or eating the
dark alive.

Bestiary

charybdis:

when i suck in / i make deadly / whirlpools / ask anyone
who's managed / to climb out / alive

dragon:

patrol or pillage / he exhales and a whole village / burns / iron scaled
sentry / guardian of the ivory / tower i wrap my legs around / everyone
thinks / he's a brute / but for me / he lifts his breast plate / for me
he welcome the quiver / and the arrow's teeth.

golem:

take his hair in your hands / his dead / skin cells / his discarded
undergarments / take them / and make of them a new boy
this effigy / his likeness and nothing / like him / breathe life
into its clenched carapace // my god / i think i saw it / move

medusa:

when i saw / my face / reflected in terror / in his eyes / i turned
to stone / or a pillar of salt watching my village burn / he was the village
burning / maybe that's a different story / maybe in the end
only the snakes wept

siren:

he cries / and i / lashed to the mast of a ship / steer my body
toward the sound / sheets bound around wrists and ankles
tears make grief / a lighthouse you wear / when i hear him
a huge wood wheel turns in my stomach / and i break / open
on / his jagged coast

werewolf:

there are many words for transformation / metamorphosis
metaphor / medication / go to sleep / beside the man you love
wake up next to a dog / maybe the moon brought it out of him
hound hungry for blood / maybe its your fault / or maybe
it was there inside him / howling all along

CLINT SMITH

Clint Smith is a teacher, writer, and doctoral candidate at Harvard University. He was born and raised in New Orleans, LA although he ironically did not begin eating seafood until he left. He life goal is to win the New Yorker caption contest, but for real.

When Maze and Frankie Beverly Come on in my House

Mama's eyes close,
she raises the spatula
as if she were going to orchestrate
the gumbo into existence.
Turns the knob so that we feel
the bass thundering in the walls.

At the start of verse one,
>she points to Pops,
>walks over,
>shoulders oscillating back-and-forth
>between the melody.
>Pops does the same dance
>he's been doing since '73—
>*left knee, right knee, pop, snap*
>*left knee, right knee, pop, snap*
>on every other beat.
>The sort of dance that has a different
>iteration every decade but really
>it's always been the same.

At the start of verse two,
>Pops drops his shoulder,
>bites his bottom lip,
>& does some sort of spin move
>pivoting on his left foot.
>When he does this it's unclear
>if he's hurt his back
>or if he's doing an unauthorized
>version of the sprinkler.
>Mama goes with it, 'cuz she's fly
>like that, & has never left dad
>hanging on the dance floor.

At the start of verse three,
>something is burning in the kitchen.
>Their hands are clasped
>now, fingers interlocked,
>swinging each other back & forth.
>Their feet are now music

of their own, the interplay between
hollow wooden floors & electric guitar.

It's like they made the song
just for them. A reminder
of the playful manifestations of love,
how the harmony of guitar &
trumpet & bass & sweat
& Frankie's voice can create the sort
of levity that ensures love lasts
long after the song has stopped.

Passed Down

Sometimes I forget there are freckles
on my face, it's the sort of thing where

I'm not always proud of my skin for being
light enough to illuminate the patches

of darkness that emerge from beneath it.
A colony of inconsistent color spread

out across this countenance. The remnants
of colonialism in this double-helixed

purgatory of a body. When I was younger
I was ashamed of my mother for the heirloom

of her cheeks, always wondering why she
couldn't just keep them to herself.

Letter From Barack Obama to Karl Marx Circa 2011

Come on, don't give me that look, Karl.
I know you're disappointed.
But to be fair you've made things
pretty tough out here.

Sure, I read the Communist Manifesto
in college, but didn't we all?
They hurl your name at me
at every rally, every speech.

Say I'm trying to take away
    their religion
    their money
    their freedom.

Right? I laughed at that last one too.
Like they know the first thing
about what is means to have
your liberation thwarted,

your agency made obsolete.
They always say you never
really know until you're sitting
in the chair yourself.

The dialectical opposition of the
Oval Office an ever-present
reality to me.
But what do you expect?!

I can't hang your picture on the wall
or place a bust of your visage
on the desk.
Who would you replace?

Dr. King?

I don't like that this is
the space I occupy,
that there is no room here
for counter-hegemonic conceit.

Everything just keeps on turning, Karl
no matter whose hands
are on the wheel.

SARAH MYLES SPENCER

Sarah Myles Spencer is a mama, poet, singer, and writer who's worked with a variety of artists, including Snoop Dog, E-40, and (the late) Davy Jones. A 2014 Best of the Net Nominee, her work appears in A La Palabra: The Word is a Woman Anthology – Mothers & Daughters, Words Dance Magazine, Requiem Magazine, and more. Mostly though, she just likes to eat delicious things, snuggle with the people she loves, laugh, and cry a lot, often simultaneously. For more info, visit www.sarahmylesspencer.com

When the Clock Strikes Six Feet

Before I was your mother, I knew the sleep of un-worry.
Loved a seamless kind of love that knows no blood or pulp.
On the morning I noticed them all dying,
One black and brown boy and girl after another, I knew we'd seen it before.
Did I not feel the swell and bulge of bruised flesh the first time?

The Second time? The third?
Is this a body burying another body inside of me?
Somewhere, another mother cries her last cry: the finale.

This once sweet earth, now wretched, muddied with rain and too small limbs.
How many dead black and brown children does it take to make the heaviest man howl?
In my dream, I watch them line up one by one by one,
Cock back their now lifeless shoulders, still beautiful, still somehow forgiving, still
Kicking and screaming. They know we cannot hear them.

Better yet, act like everything still comin' up clean, while they flounder.
Understand, only when we are buried neck deep in the same ground.
This knowing splits me clean open. All the bodies buried inside of me spill out,

Waltz away with limbs intact, carefully brush off the mud.
A song I do not recognize repeats over and over and over.
The children laugh with their other mothers, ask me if I want to dance.
Ever been in a dream where you're sure you've already awoken?
Right before I open my eyes, they kiss me gently, one by one by one.

Someday, I know I must send you into this battlefield, flushed
With taken bodies, mothers sewing and wailing; too many names stitched into the soil.
A song that is vaguely familiar repeats over and over and over,
Leaves me an emptied dreamer. The sleep of un-worry
Long since gone. My bags packed, full of fresh demons,
Oddly shaped and dressed like children I once knew.
When I was not yet your mother. When I rested sweetly, undisturbed,
Surrounded by unfilled graves.

Before I was your mother. When I knew sleep, unworried;
A tame fear. Till the day they ripped you still wet from me, and I bled a new kind. Oh,
Cock back your trembling shoulders, little ones. I am awake, wholly.
Know I will ruin, every shovel I meet, that dare even whisper your name.

The Last Pull

Sometimes the crackers don't do anything
but remind you of how sick you really are.
You chew them methodically, suck
every last bit of salt from their crisp corners;
swallow. It is hard to lie in bed all day.
It makes the body ache with longing and inactivity.
All the things you want to do float
above your head like a billowing mobile,
but no sweet music plays to accompany them.
There is only the sound of your own slow
breath, careful not to wake the thick
dance of heave and pulse waiting in the back
of your throat. You wonder if this is what it was like
for your mother. The weekend she died,
she was in bed the whole time.
She said she felt a little under the weather.
This wasn't unusual. Your mother was sick all the time.
Nobody expected it to be the last pull.
Nobody expected this small seeming flutter
to be the thing that finally did her long ravaged body in.
These days, you count the years you've been ill
on your fingers like a metronome. You wonder,
when did it first visit her? Was she this young?
You didn't have time to talk about these things.
You were only twenty one.
You fought about money, and your father,
and the raging notions of two women
who carried the weight of everyone before them
on their soft necks.
You never tell your friends this version.
How when you called her that weekend,
you hadn't spoken for two months prior.
How now that it's gone,
you never talk about how broken
this thing that means so much, really was.
She said she felt a little under the weather,
remember? And you said your I love yous,
not knowing it was the last time.
You try to push these thoughts
from your head when you curl your body
around your husband at night.

You try not to think about your father,
how his last word nine years later, was her name,
gurgling in the back of his wilting throat.
It is hard to make love when the taste of death
is fresh in your ragged mouth.
It is hard to run your hand over the smooth
skin of the man you love without feeling the silk
lining of his own coffin.
You do not dare say it.
You do not dare confess.
It isn't that you want to kill
the things you love
so dearly. You are just so afraid
of losing them
all the time.

ROB STURMA

    has done some weird stuff like recording a poem in DJ Z-Trip's bathroom, reading a poem to a hotel room full of professional wrestlers, and drinking with Spike from *Buffy The Vampire Slayer* (before ever watching the show).   All of these events were the obvious stepping stones to him creating and curating the online pop culture poetry journal FreezeRay. He also writes hella poems and tweets @ratpackslim, which does nothing to reduce his nerd factor.

Tinder

PART ONE: THE WARMINATING

One night, after we kissed goodbye,
my porch caught fire
from an errant spark off a cherry
hitting dry and wanting flesh.

The way to my hearth,
a wall composed solely
of tinder. Ready to burn.
Has been for a while.
These are optimal conditions
for things to blow the hell up.

This stands to reason.
There is no one in this room tonight
even remotely resembling the word
cool.

We are all flushed cheeks,
thanking g-d for ceiling fans.
We are hand candles.
I am drawn to you like sparks
to tinder.

PART TWO: THE HEATENING

As an addict, I replace
things or routines with other things
or routines. Sparkling water when
I want a drink. The adrenaline of
Scoville units to feed the buzz. A mint
when I want to set things on fire and inhale.

I am wholly aware of how much heat
you give off. I have been trying
for years to store heat like that
in my throat, I have spent years running
towards it. You are where I go to
when I need to replace hollow with full
and not catch fire in the process.

PART THREE: THE BURNINATING

When I met you I was the driest pile of twigs.
When I met you, you spun the zippo wheel fast.
Combustible elements who were clearly
off the charts. Susanna Hoffs tells me to
close my eyes and give her my hand, darling,
and it is now our personal prom theme.

Sing porch fire to me
and I will melt accordingly.
You and I: the warmest receptions,
the burning home fires,
erratic, dancing, tinder and sparks.
We look perfect in this light.

Lure, or Paul Heyman and I Go To Hot Topic Because It's BOGO T-Shirt Weekend

after Ellyn Touchette

Even before we enter the store,
When we are still by LensCrafters,
scream-o music throbs from Hot Topic's retail orifices,
making small children uncomfortable
and forcing old people to cross to the other side
as if these Sons of Slipknot have a posse
    (caveat: in this mall, they very well may).
Paul chuckles and says,

*This sound was cutting edge back when we had Shane Douglas drop the belt
in Philly. Now it's just elevator music.*

He's dressed to the nines (as is his way)
and I couldn't feel more like a fanboy in my Daniel Bryan ballcap
and nWo T-Shirt,
but the truth is it's Buy One Get One weekend at the one place in the mall
that still carries wrestling t-shirts, and really cool ones.
Not the ones with cartoonish depictions of Technicolor superheroes
    (though Paul and I do have a feverish debate as to whether or not
      he'd be the perfect casting for Doctor Octopus in a Spidey movie—
      there's nothing wrong with superheroes in context after all).

The display upfront is overflowing
with those adorable POP! collectables made by FunKo,
the ones that look like Hello Kitty attempting cosplay.
The Architect of Extreme raises his eyebrows
And beelines for them—

My kids love these, he tells me.

Dark Willow! I reply.

We hold up little Groots and Green Lanterns to show each other that we may or may
not buy.

Arrrgh, Paul. I can't get caught up here. I came to find some t-shirts.

I walk in to a wall of Adventure Time,
Marvel Comics,
and vintage logos from 90's bands.

The 19-year old bangled employee leans on the counter looking at me,
attempting customer service via mental telepathy.

I ask her, Do you have any t-shirts that say *"I'm a Paul Heyman Guy"*?

Who's Paul Heyman?

I look over to Paul with my head on a swivel.
He's loading up a basket
with the cutest Walking Dead bobbles you've ever seen.
He's heard none of this.

I want him to set down the basket and say

Ladies and gentlemen,
My name is Paul Heyman,
and I am the advocate for Rob Sturma and his shopping needs.
I want him to spend ten minutes dressing down
and deconstructing the terrible floor plan executed by the assistant manager.

He only sets the basket down on the counter and says,

I'm definitely getting these, as soon as my friend is done picking out shirts.
Rob, did you find anything?

Uh, yeah. An old school Macho Man in lavender and one with a retro Bash At The Beach logo.
And some Punk stuff on clearance.

Put 'em in the basket.

Paul, are you sure?

He insists because we both know there's nothing like a good sale.

The Nerd Bait at the entrance has worked.

Antisocialist

for CM Punk

One day you went to take out the trash
and someone was waiting there
for your autograph.
You're a prick
when you won't take a picture with a fan
at an airport
at 2AM.

I am not mad at you for walking out
on the action figure and video game money.

You threw yourself into so many glass ceilings
and came back still bleeding, still broken,
not whole. But they needed you, they said.
They needed you and the pop that eclipsed
the static and Vernon Reid guitars
crunching out of the speakers.

You were never a fan of going through the motions.
You saw your opponent's knees crumble bump by bump,
men you traveled down the road with
lose feeling in their arms when their necks
betrayed them.   It was impossible for you
to be the body you were before.
All the changes you were told would be made
were printed on t-shirts and shrank in the wash.

They could have at least come through on the ice cream bars.

So it's okay if you want to enjoy
what being a fighting champion brought you:
a lair in the heart of your stomping grounds.
A flourishing new marriage. A chance to breathe
for the first time in years.
Blackhawks season tickets you can actually use.

Never say never is the song on every wrestler's playlist.
You remixed it on a red carpet, screaming
never /ever/ ever

and your cult of personality wobbles.
If you listen through the edits,
your name echoes through Rosemont,
hoping they can conjure you from the gorilla position.

I wish you walks on the beach
that aren't broadcast one still shot at a time.
I wish you find that spark
that makes you want to put on kickpads again,
to come out from behind a fist clutching lightning,
to shout Ben Grimm's battlecry from bended knee.

Now is the time for you to put away all your luggage.
To learn what it is to be a fan again.
If you never return, we understand.
But we will never stop chanting your name.

ADAM TEDESCO

Contributing editor Adam Tedesco has worked as a shipbuilder, a meditation instructor, a telephone technician and as cultural critic for the now disbanded Maoist Internationalist Movement. He is currently in the process of remembering the shapes and sounds of every animal he has come into contact with since the last time he was born. He lives in Albany, New York, where he prays to rabbits with his wife and two children.

Rabbit

after A$AP Ferg

God what if all the storms of luck and trauma never lead to a God
say when the body stops we are just forgetting how to say
son I forgot the future tense of love where the body is my son
you piggy backing my nakedness draining its honeyblood to keep you
don't stop drilling inside my veins where everything leaves but you don't
wanna because you're a perfect purple emptiness and you don't wanna
go get born or go get rocked to sleep or get so high you don't wanna go
down in the amber bath of never like everyone before us learned to go down
now this is what we call the waiting room and breath its shifting clock strikes now
you call me my birth name because I'm defenseless against rivers like you
praying that we really are as small as we think we are and need to be praying
in temples of transient shimmer of gold flake poultice and petals to place in
that mouth of yours to fix its language to say the names of those in that
trap of knowledge and love without memory of what came before this trap
when the shapes mouths made were new everything was going to be perfect when
you grew into your imagination you imagined yourself sliding right out of you
hear your weightless insides leave through the fleshy eye not where you hear
that cellophane cinnamon unwrapping in echoes of what comes after that
gun smokes the room of us for the crucifer sleepwalks the censer smokes the gun
sound of blood inside the river wrapped in a blanket of leaf protected from the sound

Felled

In the morning I'll wake you early so we can burn the edges together. I soaked your map in a jar of earl grey earlier and now it's drying. Before you went to bed you looked it over to make sure it was still legible, scanning for the gold spots. Maybe tomorrow we'll trace your lines in acrylic, thicken them up?

Past the dark forest, near the folded corner, there's a blank spot where you told me something. A place you can only get to through a tornado. I wanted to tell you I'd been there. I was in the tiny bakery, when it was still part of Story Town, when the anvil formed and the tower leaned down. My mother told me to put my head down as she knocked on the tiny shelter's two-by-four frame. I heard a roaring belch, and when I peeked through the plexiglass window I saw a pair of twisted legs sticking out from under the felled tree's belly. Cinderella's horse was bucking. They gave me a free pass as I left the gift shop.

I tried to bring you there, but a teenager with blood in her hair pointed a knife at your neck, and you started crying, running to your mom. I tried to tell you it'd be okay. I told you about how I used to come here when I was your age and ride the tornado because it gave my sweat a chance to dry. I wanted to tell you about all the tornadoes I've been: pussy funnel, whiskey spout, multi-vortex of blood and cocaethylene, spinning tower of fire living with the teenage girl that held the knife, supercell of the people; people that don't live here. People that live in a place you can only get to through a tornado. They live in dung-bricked huts and pack clay into brick molds all day while you write persuasive essays and read about every species of dangerous fish. If you ask me what the people use to burn the edges of their treasure maps while eating cereal inside their huts, I'll tell you I assume they use a dung fueled fire, but I'm not sure and it's not important, because you'll never be one of the people. You'll build tornadoes.

The Odd Vein

"I've done a lot of fucked up things, but I've never put a needle in my arm" my father tells me after he finds out I've been doing heroin. He assumes I was shooting up, and I don't correct him. I don't tell him I've only snorted dope, that at seventeen, I'm at the mercy of older friends with money. I rarely get more than a line and an envelope's dregs. I don't tell him that this isn't enough to develop a real habit.

What are you taking?

The first time I push a needle through my skin I'm standing in the front of the bathroom mirror holding a 3 ml syringe, working up nerve. I'm positioning the metal's tip at various points on my ass. After several false starts I push slow through layers of fat, ignoring the alcohol burn until plastic meets skin. I squeeze the plunger down as far as I can and feel the warm scratch grow, imagining a pool of steroid forming a pocket in the cheek. When I pull the needle out blood geysers onto the wall's white tile.

Let me see.

Days later I make my next attempt sitting on the edge of my tub. I stare down at the top of my thigh, pushing the needle into what I deem to be its sweet spot, where, in the days to come a raised welt glows red and purple. I feel pulsing heat radiate out of it, even in the days after it opens, weeping through its dressing. A hard crust of scar crystallizes on its surface and spreads in fractal reaching across my skin.

Do you take drugs?

Years before this, I watch Dead Ringers with my father. We watch twin brothers share sexual partners, gaslight their patients, and go insane. Once the film comes to the point where one brother puts a needle in the other's arm, my father gets up and turns the television off. "This is sick shit."

Pain creates character distortion.

Eventually I get better at puncturing my skin. I learn all the tricks of the needle, of my skin. How to push through a scar, a vein. The quick dissipating washes of salt sting from growth hormone and insulin. Pushing muscle bound oil reserves with hot hands and walls. The bell chimed cocooning of Dilaudid's race toward my heart.

There seems to be some problem about...

...surgical instruments.

I learn veterinary chemistry. How to strip binders off the hormone with drain cleaner. How to rinse the burn away. I watch crystals of testosterone and Trenbolone form in freezer stored mason jars. I spend hours staring into these snow globes.

About holding them as evidence of a disturbed mind.

Years before I write I can extract the light of the jungle through an iced pane I temporarily blind myself in one eye while emptying a jar of Amazonian tree bark soaked in lye.

Radical technology was required!

After leaving my wife and son, I shoot a Subutex in a public restroom and wake up hours later on the cold wet floor, syringe still in arm.

Something radical is definitely required.

Months after my longest stretch of ballooning my body beyond all reasonable doubt, after running out of places to stab myself, out of places to store fluids in muscle, after I lose the ability to get out of bed without becoming out of breath, the doctor calls. I have a tumor in my thyroid.

Side effects: sleeplessness, rapid heartbeat...

...euphoria.

After a long weekend in the Catskills watching my childhood idols, spending my veins, shooting enough coke to keep my head above the opiate waves, I sit in the doctor's office. A nurse holds an ultrasound wand firm against my throat as a doctor pushes a needle into it. I feel choked. I want to scream, but am unable to. This is repeated four times before I am told I need to have my thyroid removed.

Take one of these.

From my hospital bed I ask the anesthesiologist what drugs are being administered, at what dose. I take mental notes, so as to be able to reproduce the chemical blanket being draped over my consciousness. Hours later I am sent home with a fresh scar and a bottle of hydrocodone syrup, which I drink in one gulp.

I guarantee you, you won't dream.

By the time my medications are adjusted to optimal levels, I've gained close to one hundred pounds. I deprive myself of solid food for sixty days in order to lose the weight.

My doctor calls. My testosterone levels are unhealthily low for a man my age. I begin applying a cream to my skin. I return to the doctor. The cream doesn't work. My skin is too thick. I will need to begin injecting myself with testosterone. The doctor explains how to do this.

Can I trust you to do that, or have I got to sit here and watch you?

I'm on the phone with my father later that day. He asks about my health and I give him the latest update. "It's not a big deal," he assures me. "You just have to find the right place to inject yourself."

TOMMY

Tommy Lives.

The Title of this story, which was written for a blog, is: These Computers Are Not Real.

I sit at my desk in front of a computer. The computer, the desk, and I are in a room which is in a house which is on a street. The street is in a neighborhood which is in a city which is in a county. The county is in a state which is in a region of a country that is part of a continent. This continent is part of the land which makes up this place we call Earth. And Earth is a planet which is really just a rock that flies aimlessly and endlessly through nothing which we call infinite space.

And within the endless abyss, I tap on keys that are on a keyboard, which are marked with letters, which create words, which are only symbols, which we use in an attempt to explain our experience in here, in this space. I love myself and I forgive myself, yet there is a knot of writer's block, which is resistance, which is a form of self-hatred, that clings to my mind. This knot contains the three Mes. The questioning me, the answering me, and the me that observes the other two. There is nothing to do now, but unwind this knot. Perhaps it will bring clarity, understanding, and acceptance toward the events that strung together which got me into this mess...

I close my eyes and one of me from inside of me whispers to me:

You remember so much you remember it all. You have so much to put down. You can't move your fingers fast enough as the words come from the heavens and land in your mind and move down your neck and into your arm and out of you fingers they go and type type type they appear on the computer screen. But you know as well as anyone that these computers are not real.

I process this message from me, and flash comes to me and I see...

*

I was faced down in my bed listening to the Bob Dylan station on Pandora. It was Sunday. The Super Bowl happened a few hours before. I didn't know what to do with myself, now. Boredom inspires meditation most days, which often lead to napping. But, not today. My mind was not behaving itself. I was time traveling again. No Zen could be found. Clarity came when I realized I needed to get out of the house. However, after this revelation, fifty-plus more thoughts floated through my head. I ruminated for another five minutes until two thoughts remained, which created two paths to take, each for a different a different Me. Either I would go and see a movie, or I would go to the coffee shop and get some writing done.

There was a pile of change on my bedside table. I picked up a quarter. "Heads I go to the movies, tails I go to the coffee shop," I said, in my head. I flipped the quarter with my thumb. I attempted to catch it in my hand, but I mistimed its speed of descent. The silver circle hit my knuckle, bounced off the book (How To Win Friends and Influence Others) on my night stand, and landed on the hardwood floor. I climbed out of bed, looked down, and saw the quarter had landed perfectly on its side. It was standing on edge perfectly perpendicular to the floor. On one side of the coin there was a lake with a duck, and two men fishing from a boat, the state of Minnesota, and inside the state it read Land of 10,000 Lakes. On the other side, was George Washington's face.

The fork was still stuck in the road. Neither path was clear. There was still nowhere to go. So, I closed my eyes and sent one of me one way and the other me the other way.

*

"You are going to the coffee shop," my brain said to me. I grabbed my uni-ball waterproof/fadeproof black ink pen, and my moleskin notebook. They were both on my desk. After I had picked them up, I saw my computer on my desk. So I sat down, opened up the laptop, and checked my email. My friend Jay had sent me something about how the Illuminati run the Music Industry. I had heard that. "You are suppose to be headed to the coffee shop," my brain whispered. Before I started to read the next unread email with the subject "FUNNY" I grabbed my notebook, and pen, again, and moved quickly toward the door.

I opened the front door to the coffee shop and saw the girl, who just got hired, who I met the other day, but whose name I'd already forgotten, working behind the counter. I approached the counter and the girl said, "Hi Tommy."

"What up?"

"You doing some writing?" She asked.

"Yup."

She handed me a cup of coffee. I handed her a five dollar bill. She gave me my change, and I dumped it into the tip jar.

"Invite her to the movies," Me said inside of me. I didn't though. I ignored Me. I just took my coffee and my notebook and my pen, and I sat down at the table near the window. I have a deadline to write a story. It is one week. It all started when I ran into a friend a few days before at the movie theatre. He promised to pay me handsomely to write a story for a blog. I told him yes of course. I needed the money because I am so so so broke. My friend shook my hand. It was a deal. He told me that story better be good. Now I can't write. But I can still daydream...

*

We started walking hand in hand through the snow fall and the snow-covered ground. White was there and white was there. It was also cold. I had a hat on, and she had ear muffs on. I wanted to run fast to get back inside. She couldn't run because her ankle was broken and she was wearing one of those plastic boots. We were walking toward the movie theatre from the car. The car was old, and the heat was bad, so it wasn't that warm in the car, but it was warmer than what we were dealing with now, outside. It was only like a two-minute walk. We made it. When we got inside, I noticed my hand was balled up into a fist. I blew into the small hole created by my rolled up pointer finger. I sent hot air down into the hole. I'm not sure why I did this or if it made my hand feel any warmer. I must have seen it somewhere. She rubbed her hands together very fast. Both of her hands were flat like boards, and she moved them back and forth, the friction created heat. Neither one of us wore gloves. I looked around the theatre. There was no one except for a pimple faced teen behind the ticket counter. I said, "Two tickets to the ten o'clock showing of Computers Vs Humans Part Two. The tickets sprang out of a metal slit in the counter. I pulled out my wallet and my hands were shaking. I passed some cash to the teen and she reached down grabbed our tickets from the slit and handed them to us. We walked together toward the hallway which lead down to the theatre doors. The carpet was orange and maroon. The color scheme was from the 1970's.

*

As I drank my coffee, I stared out the window at the high brow and pretentious coffee shop across the street. Why am I in this place? Once I get paid for this story that I will, but can't, write then I will take my riches across the street and tip back expensive coffee drinks with all of them. "Who's them?" I thought. Then I instantly countered that thought with "who am I?" Then both those thoughts evaporated into a big thought, which exploded inside my skull, which is under my face, but over my brain which was, "What happens if I don't write this story!"

The answer did not really matter. Just like the answer to the questions: What do you do? How's the writing? Do you have a job? What are your plans? Where do you live? How old are you? What's your favorite color? And on and on and on... Is there ever a right answer? To anything. No there is not. Answers are not real, just like computers.

But actions are real, and as the thoughts slowed down, I decided I would try to write something. I finished my coffee. I put my pen down on the empty white page of my notebook, and blam! instantly, "What are you going to write about?" one of mes asked me.

"How the fuck should I know?" I told it.

I stepped outside for a smoke, and once I was outside I knew I had to go home as fast as I could. Too much thinking never leads anywhere that good..

*

I told her I needed to use the bathroom so I handed her the tickets. I went into the bathroom. There was a man looking at himself in the mirror. I looked at him quickly and quickly pointed my eyes toward the urinal I was inspired to pee into. I peed and heard my pee hit the porcelain and I listened for the man to leave, but I didn't hear him move. When I was done, I zipped my fly, and I turned around, and I saw the man still staring at himself in the mirror. I walked to the sink and turned on the faucet. I got my hands wet. Then I put my right hand under the soap dispenser and used the heel of my hand to make the pink soap drop into the palm of my hand. Then rubbed my hands around each other. I put them under the stream of water and rubbed them around, again. I looked into the mirror and looked at myself. I saw my blue eyes, my crooked nose, my yellowing teeth, my receding gums, my somewhat of a unibrow. I saw my hat on the top of my brown hair. I thought to myself that it seemed odd that I never get to really see myself. No one does. Only in reflections. Only in pictures. Only in the words that I put in computers. This realization brought fear into my gut and I looked back down at my hands before I could think about that fact for one more second. All the soap had been sprayed away. I moved away from the sink. I looked at the man. He made a throat clearing sound that resembled paper tearing. Then he hocked a loogie into his reflection in the mirror. The spit splattered, and the main chunk hung for a second and then slid down the mirror. The man turned his head toward me. We made eye contact. He smiled. I turned and took a few steps toward the paper towel dispenser. I pulled out a few sheets and wiped my hands dry. I rolled up the wet paper towels and threw them into the trash can. I turned and saw that the man was not there. I opened the bathroom door and left.

Inside the theatre, she sat in silence. There was no one else in the room with vintage fabric on the walls. The theatre used to be an opera house. Now it was just a movie theater. I sat down next to her. She looked at me and smiled. I put my hand on her leg. She put her hand on top of my hand and then the previews started.

The first preview was for a movie about ninjas that just landed on the moon, and realized that they were supposed to have landed in China, and that it must be a conspiracy that they ended up in space, and by the end of the preview it was implied (not to spoil anything) that they were, in fact, part of a government plan to see what would happen to ninjas on the moon. The second preview was for a children's animation about a dolphin who realizes that when he grows up he will be killed by tuna fishermen like his father and his father's father. The dolphin sets out on an adventure to stop all commercial fishing and to restore sanity to the Asian nations who eat too much fish. The feature presentation started. When it ended I got up and so did she. We entered the lobby and I saw my friend. He asked me if I wanted to write a story for a blog.

*

Once I left the coffee shop, I walked and smoked down the street. I took a right onto the street where my house, room, desk, and computer are located. When I got to my house, I opened the front door, ran up the stairs, opened the door to my room, threw my pen and notebook on the floor, and jumped back into bed. "You gotta think of something to write bro," Me said to myself.

I closed my eyes and started to meditate. I began to think about why there were rings around Saturn. This lasted approximately five minutes. Then I wondered when I would find a job. Lastly, I thought about writing, and how much I loved to do it, when my brain and all of mes would allow me to.

*

My mind just came back into the NOW which is all that is real, so they say. I am staring into my computer. I move my index finger across the mouse pad. I position the tiny arrow inside my computer over the 'X' in the right corner of the word document for the story which I struggle to write. The white screen vanishes with a click of the mouse. My desktop is here, now, and it shows me laughing while at a party in a photo from the past, exactly five years ago.

I open the internet by moving the arrow over the icon which is labeled 'web.' The screen for a search engine appears. I am bored and horny and the girl is not here. I type in the name of a dating website that my friend Jay told me about just the other day.

I don't have an account, but I want one, now. I type words into boxes, which are labeled interests, hobbies, and personal information. I type what I think is what I like, what I believe to be what I do, and who I think I really am. I stop. I snap out of the trance that the glow of the computer screen, which holds the internet, has put me in. I read what I just wrote. What I read is not real, just like this computer.

The information I entered into this profile is what I believe people want me to be. Or, is it who I want them to think that I am.? How can I ever be certain? Can anyone ever be?

Me chimes in, and asks, "Do you really like Eggs Benedict? Or, is it because you know that it makes a great photo that you take with your cellphone which is only another computer. The photo travels in hyper speed breaking the sound barrier, transcending time and space, and goes on your dating website profile. That is real. Who are you, me, we trying to impress? Ourselves or each other or the imaginary audience of all of them? Who is them again?"

Okay, I'm back again. It's me again. Can I just leave these boxes blank? Can I have no interests? Can I have no hobbies? Can I have no personal information? Can I be nobody? Can I shatter this computer by chucking it out my window? I can't because I have to write a story. I need to leave the house. BRB.

*

I woke up, stood up, and stumbled toward my bedroom door. I made it down the stairs and into the bathroom. I don't remember turning on the shower, but I showered. Then I dried off, shaved, and brushed my teeth.

When I got back to my room, I put on a clean shirt and a nice pair of pants. I grabbed my leather folder off of my desk and headed for the door.

I entered the coffee shop. The girl was working, again. "Can I get a coffee and a blueberry muffin," I asked.

"You look clean," The girl said.

"I have a job interview," I said.

"Good luck!" She said.

On the way up the elevator, I felt a little nervous. I took a few deep breaths. That seemed to help. I waited on a couch in the room where the front desk is located. The secretary answered her phone. Then told me, "They are ready to see you."

I entered the room. There was a large wooden desk. On one side of the desk, there was an empty chair. On the other side, there were two empty chairs. I sat in the single empty chair. My anxiety began to start back up, so I closed my eyes. I took three deep breaths. I opened my eyes and saw two of me sitting in the chairs in front of me on the other side of the wooden desk.

I closed my eyes, and opened them again. My twins were still there. I am one of three mes. I didn't know I was a triplet. I didn't know I had any siblings for that matter. What are the chances that my long-lost triplet brothers would be interviewing me? What are the chances?

I took my resume out of my leather folder and slid it across the table. Me on the left grabbed it. He said, "You think we don't know everything about you already?" Before I could answer, the Me on the left passed the paper to the Me on the right.

"I like what you have done here," said Me on the right. Then, that Me crumpled up my 8.5×11 piece of white paper which had all of my education, work experience, and interests, typed up in courier new font. Me on the right put the paper ball into his mouth and started chewing. He swallowed. Then, he opened his mouth and stuck out his tongue. He ate my resume which I had created with a template that I found on a career website on my computer, which I bought with my student loans.

The two Mes burst into laughter. I tried to play it cool, but I could feel myself getting angry. My face was hot. I wanted to kill my Selves. The two of Me stood up in unison and started yelling, "You suck." I blinked. The Mes were now standing on the wooden desk. They began to jump up and down. They started to yell, "Who the fuck do you think you are?"

"Uh, I'm Tommy Walsh?" I replied.

"Who?"

"Tommy Walsh."

"So what?"

"That's who I am."

The Mes got on their hands and knees and started barking at me. I closed my eyes and could feel spit hitting my eye lids. The barking continued. It grew louder. I closed my eyes harder, and I counted to ten, in my head. I opened my eyes and one me was standing nose to nose with me, staring directly into my eyes. The other me was standing to my left an inch from my ear. They were silent. Then one me, to my left, stuck out his tongue and began to lick me. "Stop it!" I screamed.

"What?" He asked.

"What the fuck is this?" I asked.

"An interview, duh? What did you think it was?"

"I don't know. It's just weird seeing myself act this way."

"What way?"

"The way that you two are acting."

"So you think we are like you?" The me in front of me said.

"You are me!"

My Selves burst into another bout of hysterical laughter. "Stand up," me said. When I was a boy, I was told to always do what I was told to do, so I stood. Me joined hands with Me, who joined hands with me Me. The three of us stood in a circle. "Guess what?" Two of Me yelled. "What?" I asked.

"You got the job! You are a writer!"

I smiled, and the two Mes began to spin in a circle. I followed their lead. We spun and spun and spun. It was fun, at first. But then, I began to think about the blueberry muffin I had for breakfast. Then, I could taste the blueberry muffin I had for breakfast. Then, I threw up the blueberry muffin I had for breakfast. The centripetal force from the spinning circle of my selves and me blew the barf back into each of our faces.

*

I opened my eyes, and I was lying in my bed. I stood up, took two steps, and sat down at my desk. (That is where I am, again.) I opened my laptop. "That was a really bugged out dream," I said out loud. I checked my email. I read some conspiracy theories. Then, I smoked a cigarette. Then, I grabbed my notebook, and wrote what you just read. Then I typed it all into a word doc.

With my mouse arrow, I clicked the Safari Icon on the desktop of my computer. Google popped up, and I typed in gmail.com into the browser. I clicked. I opened my gmail. I clicked compose. I typed in my friend's name. His email address appeared. In the subject line I typed: "Story for Blog" In the body, I wrote: "Yo bro here is a story I wrote for the blog. I hope you like it." I hit the delete key, and erased "I hope you like it." I moved the mouse over the word "attachment" and clicked. The word made me think of my ex-girlfriend. I found the file named "Story for Blog" and clicked on its icon. A clear bar appeared, and it began to fill with blue. When it was done, I moved the mouse arrow over the word SEND, and I clicked.

*

How did I write that last paragraph even though the story was already done? Because it wasn't done, and I'm finishing it right now. That wasn't what I did, but what I'm about to do. My brain is telling me that it's not sure if it's even a story, or if it's done. Or what day it is, or year, or time, or dimension. Nor do I have the answer to any question my brain or anyone wants to ask me. But, I wrote something, and if you, or one of me, asked me how it felt, I'd answer, "Not bad."

Epilogue

My friend sent me a check for 1.5 million dollars upon the reception of my story. I was satisfied. I was glad that with all of the stories that my mind spins, along with all of the stories that float around outside of my mind, that I could catch one and give it to a computer, a friend, and a blog before it disappeared. I will purchase a spaceship with the money that I have made. I will get into the spaceship, blast off, and fly through infinite space. I will go rescue those ninjas that are still stranded on the moon.

KAYLA WHEELER

is a feminist writer & two-time NorthBEAST Underground Team Slam Champion. In 1998, she won Talent America, a national dance competition in New York City where she performed with her twin sister to The Spice Girls' *Spice Up Your Life*. She was Baby Spice, obviously. Follow her @KaylaSlashHope

The Year Mr. Iliopoulos Was Arrested In Front of His Math Class and Convicted of Raping a Student

In the middle of a pop quiz
a kid in the back row

called the substitute a bitch
because *he never made us do this shit.*

The junior girls started breaking
dress code, their lace thongs popped up

from under low-rise cutoffs
daring Mr. Young to send them home

to air conditioning
and unlocked liquor cabinets.

PTA moms petitioned
for more organic lunch options.

When the wrestling team discovered
security cameras hidden in the woods

surrounding the baseball field, they quit
offering to walk freshmen home.

One girl got expelled
for keeping a pocketknife

nestled between her knuckles
while she walked to the parking lot.

Another was kicked out of an honor society
for showing off her pregnant belly.

The police chief was named Hero
of the Year by the local newspaper.

Carrie stole Jenna's boyfriend
for the last time.

The janitor looked up cheerleaders' skirts
as he mopped blood and hair

extensions off the floor.
The football team went undefeated

all season. Chrissy hid her bruises
under Matt's letterman jacket

for the Class Couple yearbook photo.
Mr. Fabiano stopped

asking Brianna to stay after class
and proposed to Miss Jordan at the pep rally.

The whole student body watched
as he slipped a princess-cut diamond onto her finger

before she could even say yes.

On Finding Blonde Bobby Pins In His Bed

At the diner, he orders a cherry cola. An expired woman
wearing a soiled apron brings a glass filled with ice
and clumps of my hair. He throws back his exquisite head,
empties the glass in one swift gulp. *Too much grenadine*, he says.
Even a sweet tooth knows the curse of having too much
of a good thing, the thick rot that follows indulgence,
how it lasts like marriage. He stares at me from across the table,
his eyes, a decided jury. *What happened to your hair?*
My bangs, now a jagged veil, reveal more of my face
than he is used to. Before I can answer, he orders
another drink, says his thirst is a neglected child drowning
in the deep end. The woman appears again. This time
she thins the layers at my crown with a dull razor, the pieces fall
like feathers over ice. She places a scotch glass on a square napkin
in front of him. Gulp. Gone. When the other patrons begin to notice
and the booth is no longer a confessional and I am no longer pretty
enough to sit at his table, he takes me by the wrist back home.
When I accidentally find the golden bobby pins nestled like lovers
in his sheets, each one the color of new victory, I hardly realize
the impossibility of them being mine. Instead, I tuck them behind my ears,
pin back the destruction until he swears I am more than just a tooth
to pull, until he turns off the lights and beckons me to bed.

Since You Asked Where I'm From

after Jeanann Verlee

High school sweethearts. Cemetery Road.
Heavy metal and long hair. Bikinis and long hair.
Vinyl floors and faded wallpaper. Farm equipment slicing bone.
Tourniquet, morphine, walking again. Crushed boots
and walking again. Three spine surgeries and walking again.
Pulling the loose tooth with pliers. Spitting blood. Swallowing blood.
Monday night football. *I earned this beer.* Drunk drives home late
from the navy yard. Drunk-installing the washing machine.
Drunk-watching the game. I am from drunk.
From putting the car keys in the junk drawer then reaching for the spares,
why the maple tree on the back dirt road looks like that.
Internal bleed. 3AM phone call from the morgue.
We need you to identify the body. Accident. Bad trip.
Thick-skinned women on the arms of mistakes wearing muscle shirts.
A six pack and cracked windshield. Car seats in the cab.
She won't leave, she has nowhere else to go.
Menstrual blood. Miscarriage. Third abortion. Miscarriage.
He can hit me but he can't hit the baby.
Stiffed waitress. Stolen car. *This is all for you.*
Tool box, trash can, screwdriver with the well vodka.
Handsaw and nails and *no one will do it for you.*
A joint checking account, drained. Unworn clearance rack lingerie.
You bitch, who do you think you are?
Private investigator, police tape, death threats on the bathroom wall.
I know someone who knows someone who can take care of him.
I am from *just say the word.* I am from *say the word.* I am from *say it.*
Slammed doors. Clenched fist. Keys thrown into a field of wildflowers.
Abandoned storage unit. Backpack.
Kicked up dirt. Kicked in the stomach.
You'd be nothing without me.
Two broken legs and walking.   Away.

HANIF WILLIS-ABDURRAQIB

Hanif Willis-Abdurraqib is from Columbus, Ohio. He is a pushcart nominated poet, and the author of Sons Of Noah, a chapbook forthcoming from Tired Hearts Press in 2014. His poems have been featured in Radius, Vinyl, Freezeray, joINT, Borderline, and other journals that are far too kind. He thinks poems can save the world, but also just really wants to talk to you about music and sports.

On Joy

What I most remember about Columbus, Ohio on the Saturday night of George Zimmerman's acquittal is the heat. Though it was only mid-summer, a late-summer's blaze set itself on the city. The kind that sits on top of your skin, hungry and unshakeable. It was the kind of day where everyone sits inside next to an air conditioner, or sweats through an old t-shirt walking the three blocks to the store, like I did, right before a friend texted me "He's not guilty. He's free."

My then-girlfriend, Laura, was back home, visiting her family in the small Ohio town where she was raised. About a month earlier, I managed to fly across the country and back in 24 hours to pick up an engagement ring without her knowing about it (a trick that involved more airport running than I will likely ever have to do again in my life). I spent most of my time on the day of Zimmerman's acquittal inside of our tiny attic apartment, wrestling with a number of anxieties about putting the ring to its proper use (anxieties that I continued to wrestle with until I finally did the deed early in October of that year, much to the relief of family and friends). I had been invited to a game of hide and seek that night in the park down the street from my house. Some revelry after a day of oppressive heat, some praise at the feet of a cool night. After I returned from the store and processed the text about the verdict, I remember sitting under a blanket in the dark, right up against the loud and rattling window air conditioner, shivering. In debating whether or not I should go out to the park and try to find a release with people I cared deeply for, I considered this idea of a black male running into the night. How we seemed to be consistent only in the art of disappearance. How, even in joy, running into a cool and needed darkness could end in burial. My name on a stone next to the stone with my mother's name on it. The unused ring, still in a drawer. The woman I hoped to spend my life with, re-learning a life without me in it, and then carrying on, as we all do. I considered my father, forced to convince a nation that mine was a life worth being kept. And I wept, loudly and angrily. I stared at my hands, pushed them into the shadows of our living room, and watched them vanish.

II.

About three weeks before our wedding, Laura and I sat in a car after processing a phone call from her dermatologist.

We don't know how bad it is, we were told.

And then, there will have to be at least one surgery.

About two weeks before that, Laura went to the doctor to get a toe injury looked at. She had recently gotten back into running, and an odd sore had emerged under her toenail. I shrugged, told her that she just may need better fitting running shoes. Because she once witnessed me eat ice cream six evenings in a row, she smartly opted out of taking my medical advice, and went to an actual doctor. Her toe wasn't abnormal, they said. But the spots on her shoulder and neck were concerning. With her family health history, we feared skin cancer. So, the phone call we got that day wasn't entirely surprising. But if nothing else, if I've learned anything from Black Death and the people who walk away from it unscathed, it's that things can be both unsurprising AND exceedingly jarring. The choices were as follows: either reschedule the wedding, or schedule the surgery after the wedding. Frantically, I thought the former would be entirely reasonable, while Laura very calmly selected the latter. After one post-wedding surgery, it was found that the cancer had metastasized, and moved to her lymph nodes, meaning that it jumped from stage one to stage three. A much more dangerous situation, one that potentially required immunotherapy and years of monitoring and recovery, if all of the impacted lymph nodes couldn't be removed by surgery.

The fragility of everyone we love is frightening. I forget this often. Even after losing so many loved ones, I forget it. I forget it even as I type this, only remembering it as I recall being curled up on a hospital recliner at 3 a.m., anxiously fidgeting with the new band of metal adjusting itself to my ring finger, watching my wife try to sleep through unimaginable pain, a handful of tubes running out of her neck and arms. I remember holding her hand while she slept, watching her thrash uncomfortably. It was hard not to recall her, just weeks earlier, walking towards me through a field filled with all of our family and friends.

A month after the surgeries, after she was released from the James Cancer Hospital and I helped her up the stairs of our tiny, hot apartment, after she once again showed me the proper way to fight, refusing to sprawl on the couch all day (as she was instructed to do) and moving what little she could while I often sulked in our bedroom, afraid, restless, and watching the World Cup, the hospital called us early on a Saturday morning. Laura was declared cancer-free. Every cancerous lymph node had been successfully removed, and the others scanned as clean. In under two months, I committed myself to someone I loved more than I thought was possible, watched them battle an illness that was considered to be extremely life threatening, and then watched it be completely removed. The phone call was casual, matter-of-fact, even. I don't know why I expected the call to be more celebratory on the hospital's end, but I somehow did.

Hey. Just wanted to fill you all in. The cancer is gone. Hope you have a good weekend.

Laura has a scar that runs across the front of her neck. Naturally, she doesn't love it. Poets often try to make romance out of wearing the remains of what does not kill you. Though she would likely be a better one than me if she took it up, my wife is not a poet. While I appreciate the reminder of what came for her body and did not succeed, I more appreciate the body that is still here. The suit I did not have to put on. The life I did not have to abandon right after it started.

III.

I don't know what to do with all of the world's burning anymore. Sometimes we start the fire directly, other times we're unwitting accomplices to it, and then there are times when the smoke rises and dances above our own doorsteps, and we're just too tired to keep the flames under control. I turn on the TV and people of color are still dying. I read the news and people in Trans communities remain dismissed, remain punchlines until they are dead, and people are still laughing at the bad joke. I talk to the women in my life and hear how they're treated as a different class of person entirely. I don't have the luxury to not dismantle the systems that allow for those things, and more. I am impacted by it, in some ways, I'm complicit in it, and it's hard to sit idle while knowing those things. While being afforded a platform, artistic and otherwise.

When we talk about "the work", as writers, so many of us mean the actual work of writing. The work on the page, of course. After a year of wrestling with the fragility of my own life, and the life of my closest human love, I realized that "the work" is also the work of living. It is the work of loving others when we can, taking care of ourselves when we can, and knowing not to let the former overwhelm us into forgetting the latter. Those two different types of work are two rivers flowing into the same body of water, for me. I don't know how to write healthy and productive poems if I'm only doing one side of the work.

The only promise here is that I will wake up tomorrow and be as exhausted by the world as I was today. Sure, I may find a brief reprieve in a panda video (or, in the case of the particular tomorrow at the time of this writing, the new Terrance Hayes book!), but I will still find myself going outside to throw water on whatever flames I can, my arms weakening. I know that they will be there, every day. But even through all of it, something happened at around the end of last year. I started writing poems about being married. About my father, still healthy and living. About the friends I love and miss dearly. About my dog. I realized this urgency to archive the things that are not promised. I need the joy in my life to live outside of my body. I need to see it, to touch it. I need that outside of my body even more than I need the rage, confusion, and sadness on the outside. I know the sadness will always replenish itself. There is no certainty in almost anything else. I don't know how long I'll get to hear my wife sing along to pop songs in the car during road trips. I don't know how much longer I'll get to talk to my father with him remembering who I am. I don't know when my dog will be too old to rush towards me with a wagging tail whenever I come back from an especially long trip. I need those things to live in other places. I need to have them outside of me so that I can run into them on the days where I will need to. Surely, each small joy has an expiration date. I have touched the edges of them. I don't know how to fight against this reality except for to write into these moments with urgency. With fearlessness and hunger.

I recently returned from a college poetry competition. I heard so many brave poems from emerging and talented writers. Poems that thankfully named and celebrated the all-too familiar dead, poems that made me wince and chuckle with how closely they mirrored the experiences I had in my late teens/early 20s, and of course, poems of survival. After one such poem, beginning in sadness and ending in praise, that hit close to home for me, I went up to the poet, shook his hand and told him how glad I was that I came in the room to hear his poem. I told him that I was glad he was writing, and how beautiful it was for me to hear this poem of survival ending in joy. He responded,

They ain't killed us yet. Gotta celebrate what we can.

And then he ran off, and I almost felt my skin rebuild itself into a new device.

(Note: This was written and edited in collaboration with my wife, Laura. We both feel strongly about collaboration when one partner tells the story of another partner's trauma/illness/life.)

Do Your Part To Save The Scene

glorify the blood
  only when it is outside
    of the body and
      no longer keeping our enemies
          alive
I say this and
  know that *enemy* means
    whoever survives when
      the music is over
        when a guitar has been strangled
          to dust
we were given hands so that
we could conjure noise out
  of anything that will have us
      until morning
and there is never glory in this
  bring me the fingers of anyone who
    makes enough money to buy themselves
      a meal
off of what we starved ourselves for
I don't make the rules
  I just know what it is to see
      an entire country wearing your face as
    a mask
  tell the boys to climb to the top
  of any billboard that carries my name
  with their spray paint and
    black gloves
I know this will not make summer
untangle its endless hair and let it
fall down into November
  but I have stopped sleeping
    on floors again and nothing I touch
    makes a sound

While Watching The Baltimore Protests On Television, Poets On The Internet Argue Over Another Article Declaring "Poetry Is Dead"

I mean is it really dead did we watch its mother pull its limp husk from the mouth of a night that it walked into living are there one hundred black hands carrying its casket through the boulevard did it die in a city that no one could find until fire drank from the walls of its abandoned homes did broken glass rain onto the streets in its memory did people weep at the shatter did people cry for the convenience store and forget the corpse did the reek of rising gas drain the white from a child's eyes did we stop speaking its dead name when a fist was thrown do we even remember what killed it anymore I think it was split at its spine but I can't recall I just woke up one day with this new empty can we uproot the body and drag it through the streets will people love it again if we lay it at the boots of those who last saw it alive are we calling it dead because white men got bored with its living what does this mean for us now who will be left to bend the sunrise into a chorus how will we harvest enough skin to pull tight over a wooden face who is going to ready the drum

JOY YOUNG

is a Phoenix based spoken word performance and teaching artist. A self-described "circus-poet," she believes that often, the best response to a world constructed of ridiculous assumptions and expectations is to be equally ridiculous, leading to performance pieces that include things juggling and stilt walking. It is through the juxtaposition of perceived realities and the absurd that she hopes to unveil places of possibility, disavow the illusion of progressive narratives of histories, subvert the dominant power paradigm, and generally queer our understanding of the world around us. Basically, Joy is a queer super-poet-hero(ine)—a one person justice league working to deconstruct reality, leaving us all with shattered pieces of "reality" we might use to construct a better world.

The Queer Hokey Pokey

She *finally* got herself a queer haircut.
You know the one:
where you get a half girl-haircut
with one section shaved—
taking one foot out of heteronormativity
like you're doing the queer hokey-pokey,
trying to turn *everyone else* around.

It made her happy,
and she knew it.
We applauded her
She beamed about it—
her hair her own queer bat-signal in the sky
announcing her lesbian arrival,
though she's been here as long as I remember.

She finally felt super:
stripped of her invisibility,
empowered,
her remaining hair wrapped around her neck
like a lasso of truth.
She chokes out another gasp of "I'm gay"
when men come onto her,
and they'll believe her now.

She remember two nights ago in a bar
being black light sensitive – only contextually visible –
illuminated when I
(or any of her other *obviously queer* friends)
stood close enough.
And our leaving disconnected empowerment lines
connecting the charge of her voiced experiences
to what being queer is like.

She sent me a picture of scissors close to her scalp,
sitting ready to cut red wire locks
effectively disengaging her cloaking device
as time ticks down
seconds (3) before she feels she has exploded (2)
into non-existence again (1)

She snaps
another photo to send
and we can all see her now.

Teleportation

Every time I think about the idea of teleporting,
I freak the fuck out.
It sounds so fucking awesome,
but my feet shake these telegraph morse code messages
trying to tap my spinal cord into submission;
I have a lot of anxiety.

I think about how if teleporting existed as a viable option
it would use molecules already in the new location
to reconstitute "you" there,
but there'd be no way of knowing if the new "you" was you
or if you experienced a horrific death
as you were ripped apart molecule by molecule
as it machine rapid fired
you across space—
a technological bullet train.
It blows my mind that this might be possible.
Now "you" are here
and you're gone
and no one can tell the difference
even "you" wouldn't know—
but if "you" were ME,
you'd wonder about it
for the rest of your-my life.

This is why I need to be strapped in suspenders into myself sometimes.
I need something holding in my runaway train of thoughts.
I can feel my spine trembling train track under the weight of them.
Hand grasping my neck hoping to get a grip
on my nervous system
of thought.

Why are you so close to me? Please don't touch me. Why are there so many people
here? What am I supposed to say? Are you going to try to hug me? Do you not know
the way a stranger's touch makes my skin crawl? My body tense? My breath catch,trying
to prevent my brain's itch to escape embodied existence? Don't touch me. I am going to
say the wrong thing. Do you hate me?Can't I please just disappear? Why can't you see
me? Why am I so visible? So queer? So small? So quiet? So prone to outbursts? Why do
I ever choose to speak?
Do you hear me?
Do you hear me?

Do you hear me?

Worrying my sanity will absolutely leave me derailed one day.
Rediscovering the ways I've jumped off the track before.
Finding myself fragmented.
I get under my own skin.
It anxious itches all over
so I think about ripping myself apart—
disintegrating from the inside out.
Unraveling double helix around the thought
of once again collapsing blackhole into myself like that
when my thoughts collect into dense matter
I can feel pulling at the core of me
the gravity becoming too much.

I stand, wondering if this trembling is my heartbeat,
if my body is rocking to the pace of my pulse,
if I could just disappear for a moment,
turn myself off and back on again,
would my brain reset to working order?
Has my brain ever operated in working order?
What does "working order" feel like?
If my thoughts move fast enough
can I manage to break
beyond the escape velocity tethering them to my body?

Deep breath:

Try to feel each air molecule
(don't think about air pollution)
move through the branches of your lungs
(avoid wondering if you are an uprooted tree)
Pull each one down into your stomach
(try not to think about the air escaping through ulcers you imagine you might have)
one by one
(try not to count them obsessively)
feeling your body expand.
(don't think about how you feel you might burst)
Imagine your lungs pressed hard against your ribcage.

Try to stay there,
pressed hard into the reality of your body.
Be present.
Try to live with the anxiety.

Don't disappear.
If you do,
you'll wonder if you've reset like a teleportation victim
and spend the rest of your-my life
wondering who you are now.

Joan Rivers Isn't a Robot

The death of Joan Rivers dispels a myth I had wanted to believe:
That she was a motherfucking ROBOT.

The stereotype in her swagger,
the cut of her tongue metallic cold
Surround sound echoing across society
her adherence to a binary
that is always one side performing woman—

she was unreal:
plastic perfection,
often slinging double edged broad sword
wise cracks
reaching deeper than her would be if not for facelifts wrinkles.

I imagine Joan would have loved the anti-date-rape nail polish I've been reading about.
Color changing nail polish,
fashion that detects date-rape drugs
literally at your fingertips.

That is some spiffy ladyspy sort of shit—

I imagine Joan proclaiming it an advancement,
commenting on how women could finally protect themselves against their would-be
assaulters—
Forgetting how women, herself included, are already stretched so thin by expectation,
And Reminding our ladyspies to coordinate outfits with both potential colors

then remarking on her own lack of sex appeal.
She'd say (real quote):
"peeping toms look at my window and pull down the shades"
that her birth control (before she was post-menopausal) was simply sex with the lights
on.
I've heard others joking (before her death)
about how after all the lifts she's had,
who knows where the fuck Her vagina is anymore

Gender is just a language of 1s and 0s.
Joan must have been part robot

It's why her programs were filled with jokes reducing women to nothing but their bodies
adding in men to construct some sense of value.

This poem isn't necessarily a critique of Joan Rivers—
She carried some strange sense of truth in her sort of cyborg body—
good thing she was funny
or they would have killed her long ago.

She would have been asking for it.
The news of her death wouldn't have come as a press release.
It wouldn't have been news.
If it was, they would have commented on how she'd been wearing the wrong nail pol-
ish.
And the men who'd reduced her to nothing would be ones with bright futures ahead.

AMIE
ZIMMERMAN

Amie Zimmerman is a hairstylist who lives in Portland, Oregon, with her teenage son and two catz. Hobbies include: taking credit for the the plants growing in her yard, hiking to places that have waterfalls, and owning too many items of grey clothing. She started writing poetry after she heard Def Leppard's "Love Bites" in the seventh grade and has never looked back.

On the Morning of Your First Day of Eighth Grade

That afternoon I was trapped-- in the car they had put both of us in
and draped towels over the closed windows,
jumping up and down on the frame,
shouting our names over and over.
I guess expecting us to have sex.
Me at twelve and you maybe two months older,
I was so scared my teeth hurt and I could only sip at the warming Budweiser
sweating between my thighs.
It got worse from there.

And the time I ran away overnight to your friend's parents' cabin:
We listened to CCR and Skinny Puppy,
played quarters with the beer but everyone kept handing me their cups when they
bounced in their coin.
I drank it all.
When we drove home after, you spilled your spittoon on me.
But the windows were rolled down and the wind made my hair like a starfish, an octo-
pus, and I unfurled all the way.

It was the first year I had an affectionate nickname.
I drew peace signs on my jean shorts and was a neo-hippie
because I listened to REM.
My best friend's mom gave me a perm.
My best friend's boyfriend spilled chew on me in a car after sex with me in a cabin.

That year I scraped a lot of gum off the floor in the hallways.

I was a cheerleader.

During winter, I scuffed though dirty hay past metal bleachers across from my house,
breath pluming.
I walked through the fairgrounds across the street so I could smoke.
I pretended I was on the track team, my bare thighs pink.
I would run with them after school til the route went past my house then stop for my
cigarettes and go to the fairgrounds.
A few times there were curlers practicing with brooms in one of the outbuildings.

During the summer, though, it was the aurora borealis.
It was Yellowstone and Disneyland.

I had a jean jacket and wore men's Polo cologne.

My ears were pierced and my new friend Polly and I snuck Southern Comfort from a Listerine bottle.

Cheese curds squeaked against your teeth when you bit them.

I whispered what I hoped.

We danced to Prince in the causeway.

I loved another girl's boyfriend pretty hard.

That other night, too:

the one with so many visitors in my tent,

I visioned the tallest trees, blurred.

I couldn't imagine how long it had taken for the needles to drift from so very high;

I thought they weren't real.

They are real.

They just don't blot out the sky anymore.

Blind People Riding Bikes

There isn't a way to dissect you from my body, or I would have done it already. You know how hard it is for evergreen vines to recover from devastating pruning and yet you wield hatchets and jigsaws as if in the circus. I bought two rainbarrels because I figured at some point one would get tainted with my heartbreak and no amount of iodine can make that water safe to drink. My socks leave a reversed welt at the double knit cuff—I keep moving it up and down periodically so that you will have an obvious red-ringed ladder to climb, you will know where to go. Lovers shouldn't need marked paths, it should be about sonar range. I could close my eyes and click my way across the trainyard, across the mall, up every waterfall and not get plowed, mugged, or drowned. My hungry click finds your breast, falls madly asleep, and wakes unsown.

Jackal

The challenge these days
for me
is avoiding my deepest desire to be an antelope.
I would never survive my
own predatory instinct and would devour me.
It is well known I
have the stomach acid of
a jackal
and can pass bones through my intestines.
I hang out with lesbians and straights and
kiss squarely with both mouths;
I'll worry about it later.
For now, this is love: softly backlit
my short fur taut,
I run and am not devoured.
I am stretched as canvas and my eyes replaced
with glass and I do not see
my vignette, forever the
not yet eaten.

Made in the USA
Middletown, DE
15 October 2015